THE

REIGN OF THE STOICS.

History. Religion. Maxims of Self-Control, Self-Culture, Benevolence, Justice. Philosophy.

WITH CITATIONS OF AUTHORS QUOTED FROM ON EACH PAGE.

BY

FREDERIC MAY HOLLAND.

Read the philosophers, and learn how to make life happy, seeking useful precepts and brave and noble words which may become deeds.—SENECA.

CHARLES P. SOMERBY,
139 Eighth Street.
1879.

CONTENTS.

vi

PREFACE.

MUCH as the Stoics have been talked about, but little justice has been done to either their literature or their history. Seneca, in whom, as Macaulay says, "there is hardly a sentence which might not be quoted, is, like Dion, the "Golden-mouthed," accessible to the English reader only in antiquated versions, scarcely to be found in the largest libraries. Their history has not, so far as I know, been fully written in any language. Such is the need of a book like this. Its first chapter speaks of the place of these philosophers in history. The next five chapters give specimens of their noblest sayings about religious truth and moral duty. These I have tried to render accurately, though freely, adding nothing, but omitting much. Of their commonplaces and errors I have made out no list. It is enough for us to see what truth Stoicism has still to teach. To show this, I have given in the last chapter some of their most characteristic discoveries in one of the most difficult, but important, fields of human thought. Thus I hope to be of service to the friends of moral culture and religious progress.

F. M. H.

Concord, Mass., 1879.

THE REIGN OF THE STOICS.

CHAPTER I.

HISTORY.

DURING the greater part of the first Christian century, the Roman Empire was cursed by tyranny, profligacy and anarchy. Then reigned Tiberius, Caligula, Claudius, Nero, Galba, Otho, Vitellius, and Domitian. But with the latter's death, A. D. 96, began what Gibbon justly calls "the period in the history of the world during which the condition of the human race was most happy." These eighty-four years, until A. D. 180, were passed under the rule of five emperors, Nerva, Trajan, Hadrian, and the two Antonines, all of whom, says Gibbon, "delighted in the image of liberty, and were pleased with considering themselves as the accountable ministers of the laws." Of the Antonines we are further told that "their united reigns are possibly the only period in which the happiness of a great people was the sole object of the government." Archbishop Trench, also, in his Lectures on Plutarch, speaks of the accession of Nerva as "the epoch of a very signal recovery and restoration, a final rallying of whatever energies for good the heathen world possessed, and in this way a postponement of its fall (with the total collapse of the old order of things), for a good deal more than a century" (p. 12).

One fact about these five good emperors has hitherto escaped proper notice. They were all pupils of Stoicism. Nerva, indeed, was banished as a Stoic by Domitian. Trajan was the intimate friend and frequent hearer of Dion Chrysostom, the most popular preacher of a philosophy whose profoundest teacher, Epictetus, gave lessons to Hadrian, as Arrian, the successor of Epictetus, did to Ha-

drian's successor, Antoninus Pius, who filled
his palace and offices with Stoics. And Stoicism claims as her most perfect product the
life of Marcus Aurelius Antoninus, with whom
closed those eighty-four years of signal happiness and good government, ever to be remembered as the Reign of the Stoics.

How much of our attention this school of
philosophers deserves is shown, not only by
the success of its emperors, but by the hero-
ism of its martyrs during the reign of terror
before its advent to power. Trench declares
that "the Stoic porch was the last refuge
and citadel of freedom" (Lectures, p. 92).
Lecky also tells us that "in the Roman
Empire almost every great character, almost
every effort in the cause of liberty, emanated
from the ranks of Stoicism."[1] And Champigny
acknowledges that "all that remained of
austere patriotism and liberal republicanism
was arrayed under this banner."[2] The pages
of Tacitus show that the great example of
Cato was nobly imitated by other Roman

[1] *European Morals,* vol. i, p. 134, Am. Ed.
[2] *Les Antonins,* vol. i, p. 53.

Stoics. Let us recall the lives of these martyrs and emperors, and, if only for their sakes, those of the founders of their faith.

And, first, of the founders: Soon after the conquest of Asia by Alexander, Zeno came from Cyprus to Athens, where he was so impressed by Xenophon's account of the teachings of Socrates as to become a pupil under the successors of Diogenes and also of Plato. The destruction of Grecian independence by Philip was so recent that the love of liberty was still active among the Athenians. Unable to free themselves by force of arms, they were ready to listen to a system which told them that their freedom consisted in purity of thought, peace of soul, and harmony with the will of God. Moreover, the union of Greece and Persia under the Macedonian Empire favored such new views of the unity of the human race as opened the way for the recognition of a new code of duties, based on the obligation of every individual to serve the welfare of all humanity. These two welcome precepts of philanthropy and resignation Zeno mingled with earnest exhortations to self-culture and chastity, and also with metaphysical and theological ideas which he found rapidly coming into favor, and which were among the highest achievements of ancient thought. His stainless reputation helped to win favor for this new system of philosophy, which he began to teach about 300 B.C., in a painted porch, from the name of which his followers were called Stoics. Of his teachings only a few fragments remain, but his successor, Cleanthes, has left us the lofty hymn[1] which Paul quoted on Mars' Hill, as well as the example of a student who supported himself by grinding meal and carrying water, and never told of it until questioned by the magistrates.

Another of Zeno's pupils, Ariston of Chios, when censured for exposing his ideas too freely to all comers, replied, "that he could wish that Nature had given understanding to wild beasts, that they too might be his hearers."[2]

[1] Another early Stoic, the astronomical poet Aratus, also gives the hymn referred to, and in a form still more like Paul's quotation than that of Cleanthes.

[2] *Plutarch's Morals*, Goodwin's Ed., vol. ii, p. 369.

All the Stoics showed themselves faithful successors to Socrates by their zeal for elevating the common people. They held no esoteric views, taught as publicly as they could, and, as we shall see, readily admitted women and slaves among their pupils.[1] Organization or authorized statement of principles they had none. All who chose to take the Stoic name taught, spoke and wrote independently, without any restriction by sectarianism or any fear of loss of fellowship.

Stoicism soon showed itself one of the last and best fruits of liberty in Greece, by making King Cleomenes, the worthiest successor of Leonidas, the champion of the rights of the poor citizens of Sparta, and her last defender against the tyranny of Macedon. Plutarch tells in full this story, which I speak of mainly because it is often said that this philosophy was barren of practical results until transplanted to Rome.

But with him we come to the noble army of Stoic martyrs, most of whom were Romans. It is two thousand years since Tiberius Grac-

---

[1] *Lactantius' Institutiones Divinae,* book iii, chap. xxv.

chus was murdered, because he tried to give the plebeians their share of the public lands. During the last century of the republic, every patriotic statesman was either an admirer or a follower of Stoicism.[1] Cicero and Brutus were among the admirers, but of the followers the most consistent was Cato, whose name has been the watchword of liberty these nineteen centuries. Few of those who repeat it think of the philosophy which taught him

> " Religiously to follow Nature's laws,
> And die with pleasure in his country's cause ;
> To think he was not for himself designed,
> But born to be of use to all mankind.
> To him 'twas feasting hunger to repress,
> And homespun garments were his costly dress.
> His country was his children and his wife,
> That took up all the tend'rest parts of life.
> From justice' righteous lore he never swerved,
> But rigidly his honesty preserved.
> On universal good his thoughts were bent,
> Nor knew what gain or self-affection meant.
> And while his benefits the public share,
> Cato was always last in Cato's care."[2]

[1] *Niebuhr's Vorträge über Römische Geschichte*, vol. iii, p. 69.

[2] *Lucan's Pharsalia*, book ii, line 380, etc. ; and in Rowe's Version, lines 591–612.

So· speaks a eulogist of Stoicism. One of its most bitter critics, Plutarch, delights to tell how faithfully the last champion of the republic served her, taking care of her treasury with unfailing vigilance ; denounc - ing bribery on the rostrum, while the bought - up voters pelted him with stones; losing his own election as consul, rather than violate the laws; standing out alone, in spite of wounds and imprisonment, against the joint usurpation of Cæsar, Pompey and Crassus; and, when civil war came, forcing his parti- sans to promise that no Roman city should be plundered and no Roman blood shed ex- cept in battle. By means of this agreement he saved the life of Cicero, and twice pre- vented the sack of Utica. And in that city he died, in the stern way prescribed by the national sense of honor, and permitted but not required by his philosophy. " Nothing would be more erroneous," says Merrivale, "than to suppose that this was a principle of the Stoics, or was the distinguishing prac- tice of the sect. Suicide, in the view of their professed teachers, was barely excusable in the last resort, when there plainly remained no other escape from a restraint which denied a man the object of his existence."[1] Such teaching simply re-echoed public opinion, which had for centuries known of no deaths more glorious than those of Hercules, Lucretia, Curtius, Codron and the Decii. Here Stoicism was peculiar only in insisting that every man had a post assigned to him in life, which was not to be deserted so long as it could be nobly filled, and also in striving to train men to such courage and patience as would enable them always to fill their posts nobly.

A death more truly stoical than Cato's was that of the great lawyer Servius Sulpicius, who died from the fatigue of a journey to reconcile Mark Antony with the senate; giving his life for his country so plainly that his statue was erected in the rostrum, at the request of Cicero.

Cato's worthiest successor, however, was his daughter Portia, who was admitted to sit

[1] *History of the Romans Under the Empire*, vol. vii, chap. lxiv, p. 254.

in council with the liberators at Antium.[1]
When parting with her husband for the last
time, she restrained all emotion until overcome by a picture of Hector's leaving Andro-
mache. Brutus afterward repeated the words
in which the Trojan sends his wife back to
her spinning, and declared: "No one would
say so to Portia, for she has a mind as
valiant, and as active for the good of her
country, as the best of us."[2]

Cæsar and many of his principal adherents
were Epicureans, but Augustus sought the
friendship·of the Stoics, and was withheld
from many cruelties by the exhortations of
their philosophers. One of them consoled
the empress Livia for the loss of her son
with signal success, all the more remarkable
because the efficacy of Stoicism is often denied, in spite of what is said by Tacitus, Seneca, and Dion Chrysostom about the services
rendered by its teachers in comforting the
bereaved, as well as in strengthening dying
criminals.

[1] *Drumann's Geschichte Roms,* vol. v, p. 199.
[2] *Clough's Plutarch,* vol. v, p 327, Am. Ed.

The next emperors, Tiberius, Caligula, Claudius, and Nero, found their despotism opposed by the Stoics with a courage which often rose to martyrdom.

Thus, on the failure of a conspiracy in Illyria against Claudius, Arria, the wife of Pætus, its leader, begged the soldiers who had arrested her husband to take her with him to Rome. "You would allow a man of his rank," said she, "several servants to look after his food, his clothes, and his sandals; but I will do everything alone for him." She was refused permission,¹ but hastened to Rome in another vessel, and tried her best to save her husband's life. She failed, and the day came when, by the Roman law, Pætus could save his property for his children and avoid the disgrace of a public execution only by what can scarcely be called suicide. His courage failed, and she offered to die with him. Her son-in-law said, "Do you wish to have your daughter kill herself with me, when my turn shall come?" "If she has lived as long and as happily with you as I with Pætus, I am willing," answered

Arria. Her friends wished to restrain her,
but she told them, "You cannot prevent me
from dying, only from dying nobly." At last
they let her go to her husband. She found
him still holding the dagger, which he did
not dare to use until she plunged it into her
own breast, and gave it back with the famous
words, "My Pætus, it does not pain me."
(*"Pæte, non dolet."*)[1]

During the next twenty-five years her
son-in-law, also a Stoic, and named Thrasea,
distinguished himself as a wise and patriotic
statesman and an opponent to Nero. He
saved the life of a satirist whom the emperor wished to have condemned by the
senate, left its session when Nero's letter
about his murder of his mother was read
aloud, and never attended after the burning
of Rome. For these and similar offenses,
among which was writing the life of Cato,
he was accused of treason and impiety. He
scorned to ask the tyrant for mercy, or even
to appear at his trial, knowing that he could
not save himself and might endanger his

[1] *Pliny's Epistles*, xvi, book iii.

family and friends. One of them offered to veto the trial, as tribune. "This would be useless to me, and fatal to you," said Thrasea. "My life is finished, and I shall not quit the course which I have held for so many years. You are young, and should take time to think how you may best serve the state." When the news of his sentence to death came, he was surrounded by friends, who began to lament; but he bade them depart in silence, lest Nero's jealousy should fall upon them. He rejoiced greatly at not dragging any one else down with him. His wife, known as the younger Arria, wished to follow her mother's permission and example, but he persuaded her to live for their daughter's sake. When the centurion came to tell him that the time had come, he opened his own veins and sprinkled the first drops of blood on the ground, saying, "This libation to Jupiter, the Liberator."

At the same time, and for similar patriotism, were condemned Soranus and his daughter Servilia. At their trial she besought the senators to spare the best of fathers, for if either were guilty of treason, it was she alone. But Soranus interrupted her, protested that she was innocent, and begged that he might die, and she be left to live. Stoics as they were, the lictors could scarcely keep them from rushing into each other's arms. They died together.

Among the victims of the failure of Piso's conspiracy against Nero were several who, like the poet Lucan, justified Merrivale's statement, that "whatever there was of ardor, of generosity, of self-devotion, among the Roman youth, at this era of national torpor, was absorbed in the strong current of Stoicism." And with Lucan perished his uncle Seneca, to whose influence may be attributed the great increase in the number of Stoics at this time—the time of the missionary labors of the apostles. The moral and religious elevation of Seneca's writings has led some of the ancient Fathers, as well as of the modern champions, of the Church to suppose that he was a Christian. That he was not is proved, not only by his wavering doubts whether the future state be temporary sur-

vival, transmigration, or immediate dissolution, but by his unwavering faith that death
is always a blessing to him who dies, and
only a necessary part of the order of nature,
which has never been violated by miracles.
Full quotations will be given in subsequent
pages, showing his belief, not only in the
reign of law, but in the importance of intellectual culture, the folly of literally giving
to every one that asketh, and the right of
women to educate themselves in the highest
studies. He speaks of the rotundity of the
earth [1] and the causes of rainbows, meteors,
thunder and lightning, springs and inunda-
tions, snow, winds, earthquakes, and comets,
in a way which proves his right to say for
himself: "I follow those who have gone before me, but I allow myself to find out more,
and to change or abandon much. I approve,
but I do not serve. They are not masters,
but guides. Read my writings as those not
of one who knows the truth, but of one who
seeks it, and seeks it boldly, giving himself

[1] *Libri Naturalium Quæstionum,* book iv, chap. xi, secs.
2 and 3.

up to no man and taking no man's name." [1]

He was no Cato, but as prime minister he gave the Roman empire five years of proverbially good government, the *Quinquennium Neronis*. His charities were famous, his labors for his friends' improvement diligent, and his indignation at the gladiatorial games outspoken. [2] He lived purely, temperately and lovingly, and died bravely. He seems to have been too time-serving and fond of money for the later Stoics to acknowledge him as a representative of their faith, brilliantly as he taught it in his writings; but these weaknesses have not prevented his being claimed as a convert to a Church with which he shows no sympathy.

More consistent Stoics were Cornutus, who was banished for telling Nero that nobody would read his poetry, and Rufus, who, when sent for similar boldness to work in chains on a canal at Corinth, said, "I had rather work in this ditch than hear Nero sing at Rome." This philosopher was wont to tell his pupils, "If you have leisure to praise me,

[1] *Seneca's Epistles*, xlv, sec. 4, and *Ep.* lxxx, sec. 1; [2] *Ep.* xxv, secs. 1, 2 and 3.

I speak to no purpose." Among them was
the lame slave-boy afterward known as Epictetus. Rufus taught the strictest chastity,
and seems to have been the first who de-
nounced the common sin of infanticide. On
Nero's death he returned to Rome, and risked
his life trying to make peace between the
partisans of Vespasian and Vitellius, when
other Romans were cheering on the soldiers
as if they were gladiators. And he alone
was spared when all the other Stoics were
banished by the crafty Vespasian, by whose
orders perished Helvidius, son-in-law of
Thrasea, for refusing to give up using his
senatorial privileges.

But the last and worst persecutor of the
Stoics was Domitian. He promptly

"Cleared Rome of what most shamed him."

Among his other victims perished four authors who wrote in praise of Cato, Brutus,
Thrasea and Helvidius. The latter's widow,
Fannia, daughter of Thrasea and granddaugh-
ter of the elder Arria, was banished for fur-
nishing the materials for the memoir of her
husband, but she carried a copy with her,

and lived to circulate it freely. Her name,
with those of the two Arrias, Helvidius,
Thrasea, and their relative, the blameless
satirist Persius, show the character of one of
the many Stoic families in which Roman
virtue survived for better days.

Among the exiles under Domitian was
Dion, surnamed Chrysostom, or "golden-
mouthed," for his eloquence, which, together
with his early opposition to Stoicism, won
him the favor of Vespasian, in spite of his
having requested the restoration of the republic. When Domitian mounted the throne,
Dion fled for his life. He wandered about
in disguise, sometimes working as a gardener
and sometimes begging his way. Poverty
and danger taught him to love the philosophy he had ridiculed. At last the news
of the murder of Domitian reached the banks
of the Danube. The soldiers encamped there
flew to arms, eager to march to Rome and
avenge the son of Vespasian. The frontiers
of the empire were about to be thrown open
to the barbarians, and civil war to break
forth afresh, when a ragged beggar, who

had been strolling about the camp, sprang
upon an altar and shouted, "Listen to me.
I am Dion Chrysostom." The soldiers gath-
ered to hear the famous orator, who began
with a text from Homer, telling how Ulysses
stripped off his rags to claim his throne.
Then he spoke of his own sufferings, the
vices of Domitian, and the virtues of the
new emperor, Nerva, until all his fierce hearers were shouting the decisive words, "Nerva
Imperator !" and the empire was safe.

Thus began the period which, as already
stated, should be called the Reign of the
Stoics. Dion had his share of its honors,
and distinguished himself as a governor, not
only in his native province, Asia Minor, but
in Egypt. Trajan may be said to have made
him his private chaplain. They often trav-
eled in the same litter, and they rode side
by side in the same triumphal chariot, at
the celebration of those Dacian victories still
commemorated by the famous column. It
was in Trajan's palace that Dion spoke of
the duties of a monarch, bidding his imperial
hearer devote himself to the public service

and imitate the philanthropy of the gods.
But the golden-mouthed Stoic found an au-
dience that he liked still better in the furious mob, which was turned aside from driv-
ing the philosophers out of Alexandria by
his resistless eloquence. He was wont to
call himself the divine messenger and faithful prophet of Immortal Nature to the common people. By him were proclaimed three
great truths, which that age needed sadly
to hear, and heard from scarcely any one
else : the dignity of labor, the sin of slavery,
and the folly of turning hermit.[1]

Euphrates, who, like Dion, was banished
by Domitian and returned with Nerva, is
memorable, because, when his pupil Pliny
the Younger complained that his public duties did not leave him time to become a
philosopher, he replied, "To serve the state
and execute justice is the noblest part of
philosophy."[2]

So much has been said about Stoic pride

---

[1] *Champigny's Les Antonins*, vol. 1, p. 418 ; also *Otto Jahn's Aus der Alterthumswissenschaft*, p 51 ; etc.

[2] *Pliny's Epistles*, x, book i.

that it is well to remember what Euphrates tells of himself: " For a long time I tried to hide my love of philosophy. And thus, when I did right, I knew that it was not for any spectators, but for myself. And then there was no danger of any disgrace coming to philosophy, but only to myself, when I erred. People used to wonder that, much as I kept the company of philosophers, I never wore their garb. And what's the harm, I told them, if I should be known to be a philosopher by my actions rather than by my dress ? "

These words are recorded with high praise by the ablest expositor of Stoicism, Epictetus. He, too, was banished from Rome, where he had been a slave in Nero's palace. Later he spent many years teaching in Nicomedia. Among his pupils was Hadrian, of whose faults, while emperor, he speaks freely.[1] He is said, despite his utter poverty, to have adopted a little boy who had been left to perish.[2] He tells us himself how he persuaded

[1] *The Works of Epictetus*, Higginson, pp. 226, 298, 368.
[2] *Martha's les Moralistes de l'Empire Romain*, p. 159.

one of his friends not to starve himself to death. The example of Socrates is held up by him as a prohibition of suicide. Indeed, he says that he should tell any pupils who asked leave to kill themselves: "Wait, like men, until God shall give the signal and dismiss you from his service. For the present remain where he has placed you. Short is your sojourn here, and easy for those who think as you do." [1]

"Pagan antiquity," says Lecky, "has left us no grander example than that of Epictetus, who, while sounding the very abyss of human misery, and looking forward to death as to simple decomposition, was yet so filled with the sense of the divine presence that his life was one continued hymn to Providence." [2] The great Stoic himself says, "What else can I do, a lame old man, but sing hymns to God?" [3]

But the most famous of all the Stoics banished by Domitian was their first em-

[1] Higginson, book i, chap. ix, secs. 16, 17 ; and book ii, chap. xv, secs. 4–13, pp. 30 and 139.

[2] European Morals, vol. i, pp. 193–4.

[3] Higginson, book i, chap. xvi, sec. 20, p. 50.

peror, Nerva, whose noblest act was his passing over all his own relatives and personal friends in search of his successor, and then appointing Trajan, the very man most needed on the throne. As Dion's friend mounted it, he gave to the captain of his guards the dagger that marked the office, with the words, "Take this and use it: if I rule justly, for me; if otherwise, against me." Trajan's victories over the Arabs, Parthians, and Dacians secured the safety of the empire. Under his strict administration of justice, Dion, Pliny, Plutarch, and Tacitus rose to the highest honors. His public spirit built roads, canals and bridges all over the empire; opened a public library at Rome; attempted to drain the Pontine marshes, much neglected by the popes; and, best of all, founded the first orphan asylums in Europe, so that two or three hundred thousand children were taken care of and educated,[1] as stands still recorded in sculpture.

For two hundred and fifty years after this emperor's death, the senators prayed for

[1] *Francke's Geschichte Trajan's,* p. 413.

each new sovereign that he might be more prosperous than Augustus and more virtuous than Trajan ("Felicior Augusto melior Trajano"). Centuries later, Pope Gregory the Great, on reading how Trajan halted his army to do justice to a poor widow, was moved to pray that this one heathen might be delivered from the hell which held all the rest. But where such men go hell cannot be.

The third of these great rulers, Hadrian, was enough of a Stoic to prefer the public good to his own glory. He promptly gave up most of the conquered territory and himself negotiated treaties with all his neighbors. He issued an edict checking the working of an unfortunate one, extorted from Trajan by the popular hatred of the Christians. Other laws forbade that slaves be degraded into prostitutes or gladiators, or wantonly put to death. The provincials he tried to make political equals with Roman citizens. Lecky says that "the process of renovation, which was begun under Augustus by the Stoic Labeo, was continued with great zeal under Hadrian, and there were few departments into which the catholic and humane principles of Stoicism were not to some degree carried."

But Hadrian's noblest work was his journey through all his provinces. He spent fifteen years, marching on foot and plainly clad, through the snows of Scotland and the sands of Egypt, hearing complaints, righting wrongs, repairing public edifices and building new ones, with an energy which made the senate call him the Enricher of the World. In Spain he was attacked, when alone, by a crazy assassin, whom he disarmed with his own hands, protected against his guards, and placed under medical treatment. Two-thirds of his reign were spent in a way that reminds us of Peter the Great, but the closing years showed a magnificence which is still attested by the famous Bridge and Castle of St. Angelo, and might fitly be compared to

> ......"the golden prime
> Of good Haroun Alraschid."

Like the great caliph and czar, Hadrian

sometimes sank into sensuality and cruelty;
one of his worst attempts at the latter being
made just before his death, when he was
almost insane. Antoninus, whom he had
adopted as successor, concealed the nobles
sentenced to execution, so that they were
supposed to have perished. On his own accession, he brought them alive, as if in obedience to secret orders from Hadrian, into
the senate, which at once decreed to Antoninus the surname of Pius. This word is
best translated dutiful. Indeed, he did all
the duties of son, husband, father, friend,
citizen, and sovereign, so well that he alone
of men carries the record of his virtues as
part of his full name in history. Seven of
his successors called themselves Antoninus,
in memory of a peaceful and righteous reign
in which the Roman power was at its ze-
nith.

Its spirit is further shown by his speech
to his wife at its beginning: " Henceforth
we have no property. All belongs to the
state." At the same time he declared that
he would not remove any of Hadrian's offi-

cials unless proved unworthy. While neglecting no public interests, he greatly reduced
the taxes by a close economy, which he kept
up, regardless of ridicule. His family was
left poor, but his treasury rich. His laws
established the right of women to inherit
property, protected the chastity of slaves,
and restrained the cruelty of masters. Infi-
delity was punished as severely in husbands
as in wives—a legalization of the precepts
of Dion, Rufus, and Seneca. Trajan's orphan
asylums were kept up, and new ones for girls
founded as monuments to the empress Faustina, whom Antoninus Pius loved so tenderly
as to say that he had rather be with her in
exile than without her on the throne. Public
lectures on rhetoric and philosophy were also
liberally provided for. Persecution of the
Christians was prevented by his tolerance.
He refused to annex a foreign nation that
wished to become a province of the empire,
which he knew to be already large enough.
Unnecessary wars he avoided carefully, saying, "I had rather keep a single citizen alive
than slay a thousand enemies." Never did

he willingly shed blood. Foreign nations
submitted their disputes to his arbitration,
and his own subjects called him the Father
of Mankind.

His wall across Scotland, from the Forth
to the Clyde, has nearly perished, but of his
character there still remains the description
which a member, during twenty years, of
both his family and his administration, wrote
down for private perusal. Marcus Aurelius
Antoninus, the adopted son and successor
of Antoninus Pius, speaks with devout thanks-
giving of the latter's "mildness of manners,
firmness of purpose, scorn of empty honors,
freedom from impure desires, and respect
for his subjects as his fellow-citizens. He
did not seek to please the mob, but shunned
flattery, considering not the popularity but
the wisdom of his actions, yet listening
gladly to opinions more correct than his
own. Always satisfied and cheerful, he en-
joyed moderately what he had, but never
missed what he had not. He took reasonable care of his health, but was not particu-
lar about food or clothing. He treated every

one as he deserved, and never envied even
the ablest orators or statesmen, but readily
helped them win glory. He was no sophist,
no pedant, no mere dreaming bookworm;
but an active and practical man of the world,
able to take care of himself as well as of
others." [1]

All this is true of Marcus Aurelius himself;
for the best critics and historians agree that
he was "perhaps the most beautiful figure
in history" (Matthew Arnold); "the purest
and gentlest spirit of all the pagan world"
(Lecky); "of all the line the noblest and
dearest" (Merrivale); "the noblest soul that
ever lived" (Taine); "he preserved through
life not only the most unblemished justice,
but the tenderest heart" (J. S. Mill); "he
inspires us with a better feeling to mankind"
(Montesquieu); "if there is any sublime virtue, it is his. I know no other man who
combined such unaffected kindness, mildness
and humility with such conscientiousness and
severity toward himself. We possess innu-

---

[1] *Meditations*, book 1, sec. 16, and book vi, sec. 30; translated with the aid of Long, Merrivale, and others.

merable busts of him, for every Roman of
his time was anxious to possess his portrait,
and if there is anywhere an expression of
virtue, it is in the heavenly features of Marcus Aurelius" (Niebuhr). A sincere and schol-
arly clergyman of the Church of England,
who has written one of our best books about
the Stoics, declares that "a nobler, a gen-
tler, a purer, a sweeter soul, a soul less elated
by prosperity or more constant in adversity,
a soul more fitted by virtue and chastity and
self-denial to enter the eternal peace, never
passed into the presence of its Heavenly
Father." [1]

Marcus Aurelius was remarkable from
childhood for love of his mother, diligence
in study, and truth of speech. At twelve
he became a Stoic, and at seventeen he was
adopted as heir to the throne by Antoninus
Pius. The news of this adoption drove him
to an outburst of tears.

Well might he weep. The forty years
of peace and prosperity which followed Trajan's victories ended as Antoninus Pius closed

[1] *Farrar's Seekers After God*, p 302.

his dying eyes, with "Equanimity"[1] on his lips. Scarcely had Marcus Aurelius mounted the throne when the Tiber overflowed a large part of Rome, swept away the public granaries, and caused a famine. At the same time the wild tribes who dwelt beyond the Rhine and Danube took up arms, and the terrible Parthians crossed the Euphrates, defeated the Roman army, and overran several provinces. It took four years of fierce fighting to drive them back, and at the close of the war a pestilence,[2] which had been ravaging the East, was brought by the returning soldiers to Rome, where it killed so many people that it was almost impossible to bury them. Galen's skill was powerless. The plague was still raging when Egypt, which supplied Rome with wheat, revolted, and there was another famine, made more complete by the ravages of destructive insects in other provinces. The Germans had with difficulty been kept at bay, but now they

[1] When the prætorian prefect asked the watchword for the night, the dying emperor answered, "Æquanimitas."

[2] Supposed to have been the small-pox.

overran all the northern part of the empire,
and actually invaded Italy.

Warfare and disease had already thinned
the ranks of the legions, and the imperial
treasury had been emptied in taking care of
the sick and starving. Marcus Aurelius sold
the jewels collected by Hadrian, and everything else of value in the palace, at public
auction, and impressed slaves, criminals, and
savages, until he had men enough to lead,
himself, against the Germans. His colleague,
whom he took with him, died by his side,
but still he kept the field. Year after year
he struggled against famine, pestilence, rebels,
and invaders.

These misfortunes fanned into flame that
continual expectation of the Second Advent
which was universal among the early Christians. They publicly declared that these
were the signs of the coming of the Son of
Man and the end of the world. They zeal-
ously inculcated the book of the Revelation,
which predicted that the City of the Seven
Hills would perish at once before the wrath
of the Lord, and the Roman empire vanish

to make way for the reign of the saints. They even dared to forge, in the dreaded name of the Sibyls, lying oracles, still extant, in which Marcus Aurelius was pointed out as the last emperor, while it was foretold that his armies would be routed with disgrace.[1]

Meantime the Romans had renewed their zeal for the worship of their national divinities, whose oracles now began to speak once more. These deities the apostles and church fathers called devils, as, indeed, does John Milton. The common people thought this such blasphemy as accounted fully for all the national disasters. There was a furious outcry for the enforcement of that law of Trajan which punished the confession of Christianity with death. Hadrian and Antoninus Pius had neglected to carry out this edict. Now, in pestilence, defeat, and famine, the wrath of the gods seemed manifest.

Marcus Aurelius did not share the popular superstition, but he seems to have known

[1] *Milman's History of Christianity* (vol. ii, pp. 165-173) translates the passages from the eighth book of the Oracles.

little about the Christians, except that their
various sects charged each other with the
worst of iniquities, that their worship was
principally secret, that they thought little of
marriage, warlike patriotism, mental culture,
or practical industry, and that they hated
the established religion, and desired the down-
fall of the Roman empire, as the writings
just mentioned show.

We must take care not to think that the
Christianity of the second century was like
those advanced forms familiar to us in the
nineteenth. Polycarp, a contemporary of Marcus Aurelius, rejoiced at hearing that some
of his fellow-Christians had broken in pieces
a clock that bore the signs of the Zodiac,
because "in all these monstrous demons is
seen an art hostile to God." Tertullian,
whose *Apology* was written . at the close of
that century, declares that "schoolmasters,
and all other professors of literature, are in
affinity with manifest idolatry."[1]

The activity with which the speedy end
of the world was preached had already pro-

[1] *Writings—On Idolatry*, vol. i, chap. x, p. 154.

voked Marcus Aurelius into passing a law
by which all those who stirred up supersti-
tious fears were liable to be banished. During his absence on the Danube, A.D. 169, he
suffered Trajan's law to have its course
against Polycarp and a few other prominent
assailants of the national religion at Rome,
and in those seven cities which had first received "the dread Apocalypse," though the
bloodiest scenes took place in Lyons, A.D.
177, when the emperor was in Rome. Farrar
says that the share of Marcus Aurelius in
causing persecution "was almost infinitesi-
mal"; and Tertullian even calls him the pro-
tector of the Christians.[1] There is no reason
to believe that he witnessed any of the ex-
ecutions, and it is certain that he took some
pains to protect people falsely accused.

Rightly does John Stuart Mill speak of
this shedding of Christian blood under a Stoic
emperor as "one of the most tragical facts
in all history." It was, indeed, a grievous
error of judgment ; but Marcus Aurelius was
led by no worse feeling than excessive desire

[1] *Writings—Apology,* vol. 1, chap. 5, p. 64.

for the public safety at a time of fearful danger. It took fourteen centuries more to teach any Christian country greater tolerance. And in our own recent war our government thought that special restrictions ought to be laid on liberty of speech. The proposition that all utterance of opinion which does not violate any one's right to his reputation, or encourage the commission of any crime, should be permitted freely, has not yet won that unanimous assent which it deserves.

No one can suppose that there was any taint of persecution in the author of those sublime thoughts which Marcus Aurelius wrote out for his own support, during the eight gloomy years which he spent in the camp fighting against the Northern barbarians, while Egypt continued in revolt, and famine and pestilence were laying waste the empire. This "purest and noblest book of antiquity" (Farrar), and "masterpiece of morals" (Matthew Arnold), is full of passages like these:

"If any one can show me that I do not think or act correctly, I will change gladly, for I seek the truth, by which no one was ever harmed."[1] "It is not right that I should give myself pain, for I have never given it willingly to another."[2] "The immortal gods are not angry with the wicked, and why should I be, who am destined to end so soon, and who myself also am a sinner?"[3] "It is a great thing to live in truth and justice, with kind feelings even to the lying and unjust."[4] "The best way to avenge myself is not to become like the wicked."[5] "He who wrongs me is my kinsman in unity of the spirit and divine sonship, and I cannot be angry with my brother."[6] "Let me remember that men exist for each other, and that they do wrong unwillingly."[7] "It is peculiarly human to love even those who do wrong."[8]

The sincerity of these grand words was fully proved. In the summer of A.D. 175, Marcus Aurelius succeeded, after painful toil and much bloodshed, in closing the German war by a great battle, which was turned from his defeat into his victory by a timely thunder-

[1] *Meditations*, book vi, sec. 21 ; [2] book viii, sec. 42 ; [3] book vii, sec. 70 ; [4] book vi, sec. 47 ; [5] book vi, sec. 6 ; [6] book ii, sec. 1 ; [7] book iv, sec. 3 ; [8] book vii, sec. 22.

storm. A false rumor that he had been routed
and slain spread far and wide, and reached
Egypt, which had just been reconquered by
Cassius, ·who had formerly won great fame
against the Parthians. The soldiers in Asia
and Africa agreed to make this general
emperor. The army of Europe was furious against the rebels, but Marcus Aurelius
showed no anger, though he marched with
such promptness, vigor, and dignity against
Cassius that the latter was soon put to death
by his own adherents, who then threw down
their arms and begged for pardon. The head
of the usurper was brought to Marcus Aurelius. He refused to look at it or at its bear-
ers, but had it buried with honor. The
papers of the rebel chiefs he burned unread.
His empress urged him to take sweeping
vengeance, but he wrote her thus: "My
Faustina, your anxiety for your husband and
children is dutiful. But I shall spare the wife
and children of Cassius, and shall ask the
senate to be humane."[1] The senators were
so severe that he sent them a letter, saying:

[1] *Champigny's Les Antonins,* vol. iii, p. 121.

"Conscript Fathers, I implore you to keep my mercy and your own unstained. I beg that no one be put to death, but that the banished be recalled and the fines remitted. Would that I could also bid you raise the dead."[1] The senators were slow to heed him, until he wrote again, saying that his dear wife was dead, and the best consolation they could give him was to proclaim universal amnesty. Persecution "should be made of sterner stuff."

His conduct toward the Northern barbarians is fitly represented in that statue before the Capitol which still shows him, mounted on his war-horse, stretching out his hand to protect his captives from the fury of his own soldiers. These prisoners he took pains to have settled on reservations within the empire. He, further, took advantage of the three years of peace, which followed the suppression of the last rebellion, to forbid gladiators to fight except with blunted weapons, or rope-dancers to perform without nets and mattresses to catch their fall. Slaves were

---

[1] *Vulcatii Gallicanus Avidius Cassius*, chap. xiv, p. 304.

assisted by his laws to emancipate themselves, and registers of births opened to prevent free children from being kidnapped.
New orphan asylums were built in memory
of Faustina, whom such high authorities as
Merrivale, Long, Champigny, Suckau, and the
Encyclopædia Britannica[1] agree to think really
as loving, modest, and faithful as she is said
to have been by Marcus Aurelius himself.[2]

But his most characteristic act was to
make an impartial distribution of the lecture-
ships in philosophy—the number of which he
appears to have increased greatly—among
the four great schools, so that Platonists,
Aristotelians, and Epicureans, were paid for
proclaiming their views, by this follower of
Zeno, as liberally as were his own fellow-
Stoics. This was not because Marcus Aurelius did not love Stoicism,[3] but because he

[1] Vol. iii, p. 88, Ninth Ed.   [2] *Meditations*, book i, sec. 17.

[3] That he could not trifle with the truth is shown in all
his writings, and especially in one of his letters to his teacher,
Fronto, who had asked him to write on both sides of a question proposed for discussion. The young student answers, that
he is absorbed in reading the Stoic Ariston, but is willing to
let him sleep long enough to take one side. "But to write

loved freedom of thought, as no one had done before, and few have done since.

In A.D. 176, Marcus Aurelius took a questionable step, prompted by fatherly fondness, and also, in all probability, by desire to prevent any second attempt at usurpation: he shared his title with his son Commodus, then but fifteen, but who, according to the contemporary historian Herodian, justified his father's choice, until he was prematurely deprived of all parental control.

The enemies in the North had never been completely pacified, and their hostilities gradually became so formidable that Marcus Aurelius saw the necessity of taking the field himself against them once more. So he mustered his legions. He gave, at the request of his people, public lectures stating his philosophy and religion. Then, in the fall of 178, he left Rome for the last time. Eighteen gloomy months he battled desperately in the wilderness, mourning over the growing strength of the barbarians, the rapid de-

on both sides—Ariston will never sleep long enough to suffer that."—*Frontonis et Antonini Epistulæ*, p. 76.

cline of Roman virtue, energy, and genius, and the renewed fury of the pestilence, which finally found him ready to lay his heavy burden down.

Long before, he had written down the exclamation, "Come quickly, O Death! lest I, too, forget myself."[1] Now he said to his friends, "Why do you weep for me, and not rather think of the pestilence and the common death?"[2] Thoughtful for others to the last, he insisted on being left to die alone. It was on the 17th of March, A.D. 180, in the twentieth year of his reign and the fifty-ninth of his life, that both life and reign ended, in the camp, then pitched near where now stands Vienna, or, as some say, Belgrade.

With Marcus Aurelius perished the glory of his empire and the popularity of his philosophy. The prevalence of slave labor had so far excluded the freemen from all occupa-

[1] *Meditations,* book ix, sec. 3.

[2] "Quid me fletis, et non magis de pestilentia et communi morte cogitatis." He dismissed at last his attendant with these words; "Turn to the rising sun, for I am setting." —*Castle St. Angelo,* etc., W. W. Story, p. 18.

tions, except war and politics, all over the Old World, that not only in each state conquered by Rome, but in Rome itself, after the establishment of the empire, the only avenue to fame or stimulus to exertion left for the citizens, in their exclusion from all independent political activity, had to be sought for in the army. Such leisure favored culture for a time, as was seen during the Augustan age; but profligacy and mental torpor soon became prevalent, and increased rapidly in those forty years of peace which, during the two reigns before that of Marcus Aurelius, deprived the Romans of the last occupation which had been left them. This degeneracy made an intellectual and self-reliant system like Stoicism appear unsatisfactory. There was a growing demand for some religion which should rest simply on authority, and should appeal mainly to the emotions. Several such religions now made crowds of proselytes, which multiplied rapidly under the terror caused by the frequent shocks of invasions, pestilence, and rebellion, and the disclosure of the weakness of the

empire.   Cowards couid not become Stoics.
Meanwhile the patronage of five successive
reigns had given Stoicism a prosperity which
was as fatal as that of Puritanism under Crom-
well.   Both faiths were glorified by persecution, but polluted by patronage, and for both
of them pollution was death.   That Stoicism
perished so quickly was due, partly to the
failure of its advocates to free it from some
inconsistencies and extravagances much ridiculed by more skeptical philosophers, but
mainly to that rapid decline in patriotism,
fortitude, and mental vigor, under the great
calamities which made Marcus Aurelius the
last teacher of a faith of which the world was
no longer worthy.

CHAPTER II.

RELIGION.

SUCH being the works of the Stoics, let us see what was their faith. This is peculiarly interesting, because they were striving to rise above superstition and mythology into a purely scientific religion. Science was still in its infancy, but yet they had reached views of the rotundity of the earth and the force of gravitation which appeared very dangerous to the pious Plutarch, according to whom one of their earliest and most influential writers, Chrysippus, who seems to have died before the end of the third century B.C., declared that, "it is probable that all bodies have this first motion, according to nature, toward the center of the world."[1] Similar language is used by Marcus Aurelius.[2] His words are these : "Everything earthy tends toward the earth, all that is liquid flows together, and likewise all that is airy, so that force is needed to keep them apart." It is, evidently, the Stoics whom Plutarch charges with holding doctrines which lead to such self-evident absurdities, in his opinion, as that "the earth is spherical," and that "there are antipodes, dwelling opposite to another (sic), sticking on every side to the earth, with their heads downward and their heels upward, as if they were woodworms or lizards."[3] This latter theory is actually stated[4] by Seneca, whose scientific researches have already been mentioned (p. 25), but seem to have been excelled by those of Posidonius, who, more than a century earlier, is said to have found out the cause of the tides.

Often do the Stoics say :

"Let us ask whether we ourselves are

<hr />

[1] *Plutarch's Morals*, Goodwin's Ed., vol. iv, p. 472.
[2] *Meditations*, book ix, sec. 9.
[3] *Plutarch's Morals*, Goodwin's Ed , vol. v, p. 243.
[4] *Seneca's Epistles*, cxxii, sec. 2.

moved according to the motions of the stars, whether from them comes force to all bodies and souls, and whether even what are called accidents are bound by a fixed law, so that nothing is sent forth suddenly, or outside of the regular course."[1]

"We shall see if all things have a fixed order, and are so interwoven that what goes before always causes, or at least predicts, that which follows."[2]

"So great is the ignorance of men, that they suppose that which is most beautiful, regular, and constant, is produced and carried on by chance, amid storms and lightnings."[3]

"Nothing external constrains the gods, but their own eternal will makes for them a law. What they have established they will not change."[4]

"Cause depends on cause, and all public and private affairs are carried forward by a long chain of events."[5]

---

[1] *Seneca's Epistles,* cxvii, sec. 19. [2] *Naturalium Quæstionum,* book 1, chap. i, sec. 4, [3] book i, prol , sec. 14. [4] *De Beneficiis,* book vi, chap. xxiii, sec. 1. [5] *Dialogues,* book i, chap. v, sec. 7.

"Is it possible that order reigns in thee, but disorder in the great whole?"[1]

"Events are always closely connected with those which they follow; and all are fitted together harmoniously."[2]

"Often think of the union and relationship of all things in the universe."[3]

"All things are interwoven, so that there are scarcely any which are not connected together; and this bond is holy."[4]

"Everything is done according to law."[5]

This faith in the order of nature led to open denial of the supernatural:

"What is so foolish," says Seneca, "as to believe that Jupiter sends down the lightnings from the clouds against columns, trees, and even sometimes his own statues, leaving the robbers of temples unpunished, but striking the altars, and the flocks and herds? Our ancestors appear to have erred, but in fact they were wise enough to decide that the passions of the ignorant must be restrained by terror."[6]

[1] *Marcus Aurelius' Meditations*, book iv, sec. 27; [2] book iv, sec. 45; [3] book vi, sec. 38; [4] book vii, sec. 9; [5] book vii, sec. 31.

[6] *Seneca's Naturalium Quæstionum*, book ii, chap. xlii, secs. 1 and 3.

"Remember that he who dies is not exposed to any evil, that what makes the underworld terrible is merely fable, and that there are no shadows for the dead, nor prison, nor fiery rivers, nor water of oblivion, nor tribunals, nor judges, nor any new tyrants, in that state of liberty."[1]

"No one is such a child as to fear Cerberus, or the shades, or the ghostly skeletons."[2]

"It is foolish to pray for that good disposition which you are able to give yourself."[3]

"Praise and welcome that philosophy which agrees with nature," said Euphrates, "and shun that which pretends to be inspired by the gods, for they who tell such foolish falsehoods about the Deity fill us with self-conceit."[4]

"Since, then, our infelicities are so numerous, what should be our view but, with an unavoidable perception of misfortune, and

---

[1] *Seneca's Dialogues*, book vi, chap. xix, sec. 4. [2] *Epistles*, xxiv, sec. 18; [3] *Ep.* xlii, sec. 1.

[4] *Philostrati de Vita Apollonii*, book v, chap. xxxvii.

a tranquil acquiescence under it, to keep ourselves from the most ignominious degrada-
tion of humanity — a lazy importunity of
petition to the gods that this or the other
event may not befall us — a conduct not
less irrational than if an unsheltered traveler
in the rain should pray to escape every single
drop which was falling on him!"[1]

"First, endeavor to gain the knowledge
of yourself. When this knowledge is ob-
tained, consult the god, if you please; but,
in my judgment, you will want no oracle if
you arrive at understanding."[2]

This last passage, like that from Euphrates, is in harmony with many others, some
of which are given in chapters iv and vii,
and which show, not only that the Stoics
valued education highly, but that they sought
for truth in such independence of other
men's authority as contrasts strongly with
the credulity of many of their contemporaries, like Plutarch and Justin Martyr.

Such being the spirit in which the phi-

[1] *Dion Chrysostom's De Ægritudine,* vol. i, p. 271. [2] *De Servis,* vol. i, p. 16.

losophers of the Portico investigated the
most difficult of problems, we should look
with sympathy and reverence on their results. The most valuable of these is the
famous Hymn of Cleanthes. Zeno is reported
to have said that "temples are not to be
built to the gods," because not sufficiently
holy.[1] But his successor reared to Jupiter
the holiest and most enduring of shrines.
This lofty psalm, written about two hundred
and fifty years before the Christian era, is
here given entire, much use having been
made of the version in J. F. Clarke's *Ten
Great Religions*, but some lines having been
inserted and others corrected from the original :

THE HYMN OF CLEANTHES.

Most glorious of the Immortals! God, who hath many
    names ;
God, ever-ruling and ruling all things ;
Zeus, leader of nature, governing the universe by law—
All hail! For it is right for mortals to address thee,
Since we are thy offspring, and we alone, of all
That live and creep on earth, have thine image.
Therefore will I praise thee, and hymn forever thy power.

[1] *Plutarch's Morals*, Goodwin's Ed., vol. iv, p. 430.

Thee the wide heaven, which rolls round the earth, obeys,
Following where thou wilt, willingly obeying thy law.
At thy service thou holdest, in thine invincible hands,
The two-edged, flaming, immortal thunderbolt,
Before whose flash trembleth all nature. And thus
Thou directest the common reason, which goes through all,
Is mingled in all things, great and small,
And, filling nature, is sovereign king of all existence.
Nor without thee, O God, does anything happen in the world,
Or the divine, ethereal heaven, or the ocean,
Save only what the wicked do in their folly.
But thou also art able to bring to order that which is mon-
    strous,
Giving form to that which is formless, and turning discordant
    to friendly.
So bringest thou all things to unity, the good with the evil;
That thus there is one eternal reason in all things,
Which the wicked of mortals flee from, and yet leave active—
Ill-fated ones, who long to possess what is useful,
But will not see, nor hear, that law universal of God,
To follow which heartily giveth a life that is noble.
But they rush this way and that, without virtue :
Some with desires of glory ungovernable ;
Others intent upon craft, which is in nowise becoming ,
And others on license and bodily pleasure—
All hastening, in fact, to something different from what they
    desire.
But do thou, O Zeus, all-bestower, cloud-compeller,
Ruler of thunder, guard men from sad error '
Father, free the soul from clouds, and grant that we follow

That purpose, conforming to which thou rulest all things
  with justice;
That we, being honored, may honor thee in return,
Chanting thy mighty deeds, as is proper for mortals:
For nothing for men or for gods can be better
Than ever rightly to honor the law universal!![1]

A fit conclusion may be found in these lines of its author, often quoted by Epictetus:

O Zeus and Destiny! 'tis yours to lead;
I follow gladly by the path decreed;
And though reluctant were my coward-will,
I none the less should have to follow still.

Similar in spirit is the declaration of Chrysippus, that fear of the gods is not the best restraint from sin;[2] and of Cicero, in his statement, made 45 B.C., of the views of the early Stoics, that "it is the universal opinion of all philosophers that God never is angry nor does any harm."[3]

Indeed, the founders of Stoicism spoke so plainly, that we need not suspect that any outside influences prompted their successors

[1] A free translation of this hymn will be found in the Appendix.

[2] *Denis' Histoire des Theories Morales*, vol. 1, p. 362.

[3] *De Officiis*, book iii, chap. xxviii, sec. 4.

to use similar language, specimens of which will now be given:

"What is God? The mind of the universe. What is he? All that you see, and all that you do not see."[1]

"Guide and guardian of the universe; soul and spirit of the world; builder and master of so great a work—to him all names belong. Would you call him Destiny? You will not err: cause of causes, on him all depends. Had you rather say Providence? This will be right: by his plan the world is watched over, so that it goes safely through its motions. Or Nature? This title does him no wrong: of him are all things born, and in him we live. Or Universe? You are not mistaken: he is all that we see, wholly present in every part, and sustaining all things."[2]

"The universe is matter and God."[3]

"What is Nature but God—that divine reason which is united to every part of the universe? Neither can Nature exist without

---

[1] *Seneca's Naturalium Quæstionum,* book i, prol., sec. 13; [2] book ii, chap. xlv, secs. 1 and 3. [3] *Epistles,* lxv, sec. 23.

God, nor God without Nature. These two are one, and disagree not in their works."[1]

"What is the difference whether we deny or misrepresent the gods?"[2]

"Religion worships; superstition blasphemes."[3]

"Never do the gods repent of their first intentions."[4]

"Perfect beings have no power to do harm."[5]

"The immortal gods are neither willing nor able to harm us."[6]

"God is satisfied with being loved and honored, and fear cannot be mixed with love."[7]

"No sane man fears the gods."[8]

"No one has known God; many think ill of him, and he harms them not."[9]

"To rage against heaven is no sacrilege, but labor lost."[10]

---

[1] *Seneca's De Beneficiis*, book iv, chap. vii, sec. 1; chap. viii, sec 2. [2] *Epistles*, cxxiii, sec. 16. [3] *De Clementia*, book ii, chap. v, sec. 1. [4] *De Benef.*, book vi, chap. xxiii, sec. 1 [5] *Ep.* lxxv, sec. 17. [6] *Dialogues*, book iv, chap. xxvii, sec 1. [7] *Ep.* xlvii, sec. 18. [8] *De Benef.*, book iv, chap. xix, sec. 1. [9] *Ep.* xxxi, sec. 10. [10] *Dial.*, book vii, chap. xxvii, sec. 1.

"Little is to be feared from man, and nothing from God." [1]

"According to our own vices, have we believed about the gods." [2]

"Let us forbid the lighting of lamps on the Sabbath; for neither do gods need the light nor men like the smoke." [3]

"He who is at peace with himself is at peace with all the gods." [4]

"Like the best of parents, who smile at the reproaches of their children, the gods do not cease to heap their bounty on him who denies its source, but distribute blessings among all the nations by impartial laws; for all their power is to do good, and mildly do they bear with the errors of wandering souls." [5]

"There is no pure soul in which God is not." [6]

"The gods are kind, because kindness is their nature. It is a mistake to think that they can harm any one; for they are no

[1] *Seneca's De Beneficiis*, book vii, chap. i, sec. 7; [2] book vii, chap. ii, sec. 3. [3] *Epistles*, xcv, sec. 47 ; [4] *Ep.* cx, sec. 1. [5] *De Benef.*, book vii, chap. xxxi, sec. 4. [6] *Ep.* lxxiii, sec. 16.

more able to cause than to receive injury." [1]

"Worship of the gods is to acknowledge, not only that they are, but that they are great and good; for, without goodness, greatness cannot be. Would you have their favor? Be virtuous. He who imitates them worships them sufficiently." [2]

"God seeks no servants, but himself serves the human race, being always near each one of us." [3]

"From God derived, to God by nature joined,
We act the dictates of his mighty mind;
And tho' the priests are mute, and temples still,
God never wants a voice to speak his will.
Then, when he formed and gave us to be men,
He gave us all our useful knowledge then.
Is there a place that God would choose to love
Beyond this earth, the seas, yon heaven above,
And virtuous minds, the noblest throne for Jove?
Why seek we further, then? Behold around,
How all thou seest does with the God abound—
Jove is alike in all, and always to be found." [4]

"Thou needest not fear to pass away

[1] *Seneca's Epistles*, xcv, sec. 49; [2] *Ep*. xcv, sec. 50; [3] *Ep*. xcv, sec. 47.

[4] *Lucan's Pharsalia*, book ix, lines 570–580, in the Latin; 970–1000, in Rowe's version.

from among men, if there are gods, for they will bring no evil upon thee."[1]

"Thou wilt find that whatever happens takes place justly, and as if done by some one who distributes all things according to desert."[2]

"Always think of the universe as one living being, having one body and one soul."[3]

"Worship the best part of the universe— that which uses and directs all the rest."[4]

"The spiritual power is everywhere, and as ready as the air to fill him who will take it in."[5]

The Stoics were pantheists, but it was a pantheism that never was seized upon by either mysticism or egotism. How uniformly all individual and personal interests were subordinated to universal ones the following quotations will but imperfectly show, since they have been selected out of an immense mass of exhortations to philanthropy simply

[1] *Marcus Aurelius' Meditations*, book ii, sec. 11; [2] book iv, sec. 10; [3] book iv, sec. 40; [4] book v, sec. 21; [5] book viii, sec. 54.

on account of the stress they lay on the fact that this is the true service of God:

"We say that a kindness has been thrown away; but what we have offered to the gods is not lost, and kindness, even to the ungrateful, is a holy offering."[1]

"The immortal gods are not hindered by our neglect and impiety from pouring out their kindness upon us. They fulfill their own nature, and help all men—even those who acknowledge not their gifts. Let us imitate them, as far as human nature permits, and give freely."[2]

"My kindness is not returned. How shall I act? Like the gods, most bountiful authors of all things, who begin to bless us in our ignorance, and keep on doing so in our ingratitude."[3]

> "But let us for the gods a gift prepare,
> Which the great man's great chargers cannot bear:
> A soul where laws, both human and divine,
> In practice more than speculation shine—

[1] *Seneca's De Beneficiis*, book vii, chap. xxix, sec. 1; [2] book i, chap. i, sec. 9; [3] book vii, chap. xxxi, sec. 2.

A genuine virtue of a vigorous kind,
Pure in the last recesses of the mind—
When with such offerings to the gods I come,
A cake thus given is worth a hecatomb."[1]

"Remember that the gods do not wish to be flattered, but to have every reasoning being act as they do."[2]

"Worship the gods, and help men. Life is short, and all its fruit is piety and philanthropy."[3]

"Thou wilt not do thy duty, either toward men, if thou neglect the gods, or toward the gods, if thou neglect men."[4]

"He who is unjust is impious. Universal Nature has made all reasoning beings for each other, to help one another, as is deserved, but to do no harm in any way; and he who transgresses her will sins against the most venerable of the gods."[5]

Other utterances of the Stoic philanthropy will be found later (see chapter v); but we must next look at the proof that it was

[1] *Persius' Second Satire*, closing lines in Dryden's version.
[2] *Marcus Aurelius' Meditations*, book x, sec. 8; [3] book vi, sec. 30; [4] book iii, sec. 13; [5] book ix, sec. 1.

founded on faith in the goodness, not only of God, but of human nature. With passages to this effect on pages 145–47 and 170–79 should be compared the following :

"No one ever departed from the law of Nature, and put off his manhood, so much as to be led into sin by badness of heart ; even those who do not follow Virtue see her, for she sends forth her light into every soul."[1]

"Never can virtue be extinguished so entirely as not to leave any trace."[2]

"Every man has power to make himself happy."[3]

"Nature has given to all men the foundations and germs of virtue."[4]

"Nothing is so difficult that the soul of man cannot conquer it ; nor are any of the passions so savage and lawless as not to yield to discipline. Whatever she has demanded of herself she has attained."[5]

"No disease of the soul is incurable, and

---

[1] *Seneca's De Beneficiis,* book iv, chap. xvii, secs. 3 and 4; [2] book vii, chap. xix, sec. 5. [3] *Dialogues,* book xii, chap. v, sec. 1. [4] *Epistles,* cviii, sec. 8. [5] *Dial.,* book iv, chap. xii, secs. 3 and 4.

Nature, who has made us to be virtuous, will help us become so if we choose. Nor is the way to virtue difficult, but easy is the journey to a happy life."[1]

"As the body is made to stand upright, so the soul is formed by nature for expanding freely, and having the same will as the gods. She does not struggle upward by a strange road, but goes back in that path by which she came forth."[2]

"So grand and noble is the mind of man, that it accepts no limits, except those which belong also to God."[3]

"We follow our natural disposition when we do good."[4]

"Mighty is virtue to win the hearts of men; her beauty fills their souls, and they are carried away by admiration of her brightness."[5]

"Know that nothing is more docile than the soul of man."[6]

[1] *Seneca's Dialogues*, book iv, chap. xiii, secs. 1 and 2.
[2] *Epistles*, xcii, secs. 30 and 31; [3] *Ep.* cii, sec. 21; [4] *Ep.* cix, sec. 12. [5] *De Beneficiis*, book iv, chap xxii, sec. 2.
[6] *Epictetus' Discourses*, book iv, chap. ix, sec. 16.

"God has placed some things in our own power, and especially that in which he himself is happy: the right use of all perceptions. Here is freedom, happiness, peace, and strength, and here also is justice, temperance, and every virtue. These we should strive for with all our might, but, in all other respects, submit to what the universe brings." [1]

"Pleasure is not, in itself, the natural state of man, but merely a result of those things which are his nature, namely: justice, temperance, and liberty." [2]

"Purity is part of the nature of man." [3]

"It is peculiarly human to love even those who do wrong." [4]

"It is ignorantly and involuntarily that men sin." [5]

"It is a part of thine own constitution, as well as of the nature of man, to do philanthropic acts." [6]

---

[1] *Epictetus' Fragments*, clxix (Didot); [2] *Frag.*, lii (Didot); [3] *Discourses*, book iv, chap. xi, sec. 1.

[4] *Marcus Aurelius' Meditations*, book vii, sec. 22; [5] book xi, sec. 18, and some thirty other passages; [6] book viii, sec. 12, and other passages.

Thus firmly did the last of the Stoics hold their original belief that "nothing is more natural to man than kindness."[1] To show fully the lofty character of their religion, however, it is only necessary further to quote a few of the passages, which prove that it was as far from pessimism as from misanthropy, and that it did not permit either discontent with the present, or anxiety about the future :

` "No evil can happen to the good."[2]

"Calm and fearless pleasure is his who knows the laws of God and man, and rejoices in the present, without depending on the future."[3]

"I prefer those who meet Death without hatred of life, and admit him without inviting him"[4]

"A good man will feel the utmost piety toward the gods, and, therefore, he will bear with an even temper whatever happens, know-

---

[1] *Cicero's De Officiis*, book i, chap. iv, sec. 2.
[2] *Seneca's Dialogues*, book i, chap. ii, sec. 1. [3] *De Beneficiis*, book vii, chap. ii, sec. 4. [4] *Epistles*, xxx, sec. 15.

ing that it takes place under that divine law by which all things come to pass." [1]

"If we are anxious about the future, it is because we do not use the present." [2]

"He is noble who commits himself to God ; but he is base and vile who struggles and thinks ill of the order of the universe, and wishes to improve his gods instead of himself." [3]

"God has given us power to bear everything without being either degraded or crushed." [4]

"Set your hopes on riches, health, office, honors, friends, children, or anything else not in your own power, and you will be unfortunate. Set your hopes on the gods, give yourself to them, let them rule you, be in harmony with them, and how can you be unhappy ?" [5]

"When death comes upon me, it will be enough for me if I can raise my hands to

[1] *Seneca's Epistles*, lxxvi, sec. 23; [2] *Ep.* ci, sec. 9; [3] *Ep.* cvi, sec. 12.

[4] *Epictetus' Discourses*, book i, chap. vi, sec. 40; [5] book ii, chap. xvii, sec. 24.

God and say : 'The powers thou gavest me,
of learning and following thy ways, I have
not neglècted ; nor have I dishonored thee.
Have I ever found fault with thee, or wished
that events would take place otherwise ? I
thank thee for having created me, and given
me so many gifts. I am satisfied with the
time that I have had them. Receive them
back again, and allot them as thou choosest.
They were all thine, and given me by thee.'"[1]

"All which Universal Nature produces, and
finds support in, is good for each one of her
parts. Be firm in this faith, and give up
thirsting after books, that thou mayest die
without murmuring, truly cheerful, and heartily thankful to the gods."[2]

"What can guide us ? One thing, arid
only one—Philosophy. And that consists in
keeping the divinity within us free from harm,
superior to pain or pleasure ; doing nothing
aimlessly or falsely; needing not that others
should do this, or leave that undone ; ac-

[1] *Epictetus' Discourses*, book iv, chap. x, secs. 14, 15, 16.
[2] *Marcus Aurelius' Meditations*, book ii, sec. 3.

cepting all that happens as coming from that source whence we came ourselves; and, finally, waiting calmly for death, as nothing but a change into the first principles of life."[1]

"It is the mark of a good man to love whatever befalls him, and to journey to the end of life, pure, peaceful, ready to depart, and resigning himself freely to his own fate."[2]

"Thou canst have everything thou wishest, if thou wilt forget the past, trust the future to Providence, and direct the present according to justice and piety—the piety of loving thy lot.[3]

"Live with the gods; and it is living with them to show them constantly a soul which is contented with whatever is allotted her, and which does the will of that guide given us by Jupiter, and a portion of himself, namely, the reason, which is in each one of us."[4]

> "With my wish all things are in harmony,
> Which harmonize, O Universe, with thee.

[1] *Marcus Aurelius' Meditations*, book ii, sec. 17; [2] book iii, sec. 16; [3] book xii, sec. 1; [4] book v, sec. 27.

Of naught as late or early I complain
Which forms a link in thy well-ordered chain.
Good fruit for me is all thy seasons bring,
O Nature.   All things from thy plenty spring,
All live in thee.   All turn to thee again." [1]

[1] *Marcus Aurelius' Meditations*, book IV, sec. 23.

CHAPTER III.

MAXIMS OF SELF-CONTROL.

SUCH a religion was peculiarly well adapted to produce precepts, of which specimens will here be given, under the heads, successively, of Equanimity, Courage, Forbearance, Temperance, Purity, and Self-Respect.

EQUANIMITY.

"The wise man needs much, but wants nothing; the fool needs nothing, but wants everything."[1]

"Fight fortune with thine own weapons,

---

[1] *Chrysippus*, quoted in *Seneca's Epistles*, ix, sec. 14.

for she will give thee none which can be used against herself."[1]

"He is king who fears nothing and longs for nothing. Everyone may give himself the kingdom of noble thoughts."[2]

"Never can there be courage where there is not peace."[3]

"What we bear is not so important as how we bear it."[4]

"The good man bears calmly much that is not evil, except to those that take it ill."[5]

"He yields to destiny, and consoles himself by knowing that he is carried along with the universe."[6]

"We become happy by not needing happiness."[7]

"Fortune conquers us, unless she is conquered utterly."[8]

"He is free who arises above all injuries, and finds all his joys within himself."[9]

---

[1] *Posidonius*, quoted in *Seneca's Epistles*, cxiii, sec. 28.
[2] Chorus in the *Thyestes*, probably written by Seneca, line 388.
[3] Speech of Medea, in the *Tragedy*, so called, and attributed to Seneca, line 161.   [4] *Dialogues*, book i, chap. ii, sec. 4;   [5] book i, chap. iv, sec. 16;   [6] book i, chap. v, sec. 8;   [7] book i, chap. vi, sec. 5;   [8] book ii, chap. xv, sec. 3;   [9] book ii, chap. xix, sec. 2.

"There is nothing grand that is not also calm." [1]

"Wisdom shows her strength by her peace amid trouble, like an army encamped in safety in a hostile land." [2]

"In the upper air there is neither cloud nor storm, and so in the lofty soul there is always peace." [3]

"Peace of mind comes by meditating diligently over wise maxims, by doing our duty, and by setting our hearts on what is noble." [4]

"What madness to be dragged along by the divine will, rather than follow it!" [5]

"Fear and penitence for those who can neither rule nor obey their desires." [6]

"It is better to look at common customs and vices calmly, without either laughing or weeping, since the former is a cruel pleasure, and the latter an endless grief." [7]

"He who is not mad with avarice or sensuality, the destroyers of all things, knows

---

[1] *Seneca's Dialogues,* book iii, chap. xxi, sec. 4; [2] book ii, chap. iv, sec. 3; [3] book v, chap vi, sec. 1; [4] book v, chap. xli, sec. 2; [5] book vii, chap. xv, sec. 6; [6] book ix, chap. ii, sec. 8; [7] book ix, chap. xv, sec. 5.

that there is no real evil in Poverty. She will not harm him who despises superfluities, and she will do good to him who covets them, for she will heal him against his will."[1]

"A very little can satisfy our necessities, but nothing our desires."[2]

"He who longs to wear gold and purple is poor, not by fortune's fault, but by his own."[3]

"Nothing is so honorable as a great soul; but that soul is not great which can be shaken by either fear or grief."[4]

"The wise man will always know how to help the suffering. But sorrow prevents us from making distinctions, finding out what is useful, avoiding what is dangerous, and deciding what is just; and, therefore, he will not himself yield to sorrow. He will do everything that could be done by the sympathetic, but he will do it calmly and cheerfully."[5]

"What is noble? To be able to bear

[1] *Seneca's Dialogues*, book xii, chap. x, secs. 1 and 3; [2] book xii, chap. x, sec. 11; [3] book xii, chap. xi, sec. 2. [4] *De Clementia*, book ii, chap. v, sec. 4; [5] book ii, chap. vi, sec. 1.

adversity contentedly, taking whatever happens, as if we had wished for it; as, indeed, we should have done, since all things happen by the will of God. To weep or complain is to rebel." [1]

"The best proof that thy soul is calm is thy ability to continue in thine own company." [2]

"Where there is contentment there is no poverty. It is not he who has little, but he who desires more, that is poor." [3]

"Soldiers have gone without everything, and eaten roots and things we may not name, in order that some one else may reign over them; and can any man hesitate about enduring poverty, that he may set free his soul?" [4]

"Which had you rather give up—yourself, or some of your troubles?" [5]

"He has reached the height of wisdom who knows what to rejoice in, and does not place his happiness in another's power." [6]

---

[1] *Seneca's Naturalium Quæstionum,* book iii, præf., sec. 12. [2] *Epistles,* ii, sec. 1; [3] *Ep.* ii, sec. 6; [4] *Ep.* xvii, sec. 7; [5] *Ep.* xix, sec. 4; [6] *Ep.* xxiii, sec. 2.

"He has reached the supreme good who is never sad, or excited by hope, but keeps an even and happy frame of mind by day and night."[1]

"Whom am I to conquer? Not the Persians, nor the distant Medes, nor the warlike tribes who dwell beyond Dacia, but avarice, ambition, and fear of death, who subdue the conquerors of the nations."[2]

"The wise man's joy is woven so well as not to be broken by any accident."[3]

"Take care not to make your pain greater by your complaints. If you will say, 'It is nothing,' or, at least, 'It is slight, and about to cease,' you will make it what you think it."[4]

"Fortune has not such long arms as we think; she seizes on no one who is not clinging to her."[5]

"What is really evil? To yield to what is called so, and give up our liberty, which ought to be kept at every cost. Farewell,

---

[1] *Seneca's Epistles,* lix, sec. 14; [2] *Ep.* lxxi, sec. 37; [3] *Ep.* lxxii, sec. 4; [4] *Ep.* lxxviii, sec. 13; [5] *Ep.* lxxxii, sec. 5.

freedom, if we do not scorn everything that would enslave us!"[1]

"Never is the soul grander than when she rises above all that is foreign to her, so as to find her peace in fearing nothing, and her wealth in coveting nothing."[2]

"Liberty is not to be had gratis; if she be worth much to us, all things else will have little value."[3]

"The grandest of empires is to rule one's self."[4]

"Philosophy will give us the greatest of blessings—freedom from regret."[5]

"That which satisfies us is never too little, and that which does not is never much."[6]

"This is grand, to act always like the same man."[7]

"My country is wherever I am happy; and that depends on the man, not the place."[8]

"Who has most? He who desires least."[9]

---

[1] *Seneca's Epistles*, lxxxvi, sec. 28; [2] *Ep.* lxxxvii, sec. 3; [3] *Ep.* civ, sec. 34; [4] *Ep.* cxiii, sec. 30; [5] *Ep.* cxv, sec. 18; [6] *Ep.* cxix, sec. 7; [7] *Ep.* cxx, sec. 22. [8] *De Remediis*, chap. viii, sec. 2. [9] *De Moribus*, sec. 46.

"The poor man much, the miser all things, needs;
Unkind to all, but worst for him his deeds.
That mortal needs the least who least desires;
He has his wish who, as he needs, aspires." [1]

"Snow-white old age comes to the patient." [2]

"Sickness is a hindrance to the body, but not to the will, unless that yields." [3]

"If a little oil be spilt, or a little wine stolen, say to yourself, 'This is the price of tranquillity and peace; nothing is to be had without cost." [4]

"Everything has two handles, and can be carried by one of them, but not by the other." [5]

"He who has learned that prosperity and peace consist in not missing what we seek, or suffering what we shun, keeps down his desires, and shuns only what he can avoid." [6]

"Whoever shuns, or desires, what is not in his own power, cannot be either faithful or free." [7]

[1] Quotations in *Seneca's Epistles*, cviii, secs. 9 and 11.
[2] *Hercules Furens*, probably by Seneca, line 198.
[3] *Epictetus' Enchiridion*, chap. ix; [4] chap. xii, sec. 2; [5] chap. xliii. [6] *Discourses*, book i, chap. iv, sec. 1; [7] book i, chap. iv, sec. 19.

"Why should I care what happens, while my soul is above it?"[1]

"This is education, to learn to wish that things should happen as they do."[2]

"The essence of good and evil lies in the direction of the will, for which all outward things are means to help it reach its own evil or good."[3]

"If you choose to keep your will in harmony with nature you are safe and free from care."[4]

"Show me some one who is sick, in danger, disgraced, dying, but yet happy. Show him, for I long to see a Stoic!"[5]

"The child who tries to take too many nuts and figs out of a jar with a narrow mouth, so that his hand is caught, must drop some to get out the rest. Have but few wants, and they will be supplied."[6]

"He bears a fever well who blames neither God nor man, and does not trouble him-

---

[1] *Epictetus' Discourses*, book i, chap. vi, sec. 29; [2] book i, chap. xii, sec. 15; [3] book i, chap. xxix, secs. 1 and 2; [4] book ii, chap. ii, sec. 2; [5] book ii, chap. xix, sec. 24; [6] book iii, chap. ix, sec. 22.

self about what may happen, but awaits death nobly." [1]

"If you see anybody wail and complain, call him a slave, though he be clad in purple." [2]

"Freedom is not gained by satisfying, but by restraining, our desires." [3]

"Of what use is your reading, if it does not give you peace?" [4]

"Not only ambition and avarice, but even desire of ease, of quiet, of travel, or of learning, may make us base, and take away our liberty." [5]

"Rejoice in what you have, and like whatever time brings." [6]

"Wherever I go, it will be well with me, as it has been here, and on account not of the place, but of the principles which I shall carry away with me. They are all my property, and they will be all I shall need, wherever I may be." [7]

[1] *Epictetus' Discourses*, book iii, chap. x, sec. 13; [2] book iv, chap. i, sec. 57; [3] book iv, chap. i, sec. 175; [4] book iv, chap. iv, sec. 4; [5] book iv, chap. iv, sec. 1; [6] book iv, chap. iv, sec. 45; [7] book iv, chap. vii, sec. 14.

"Ask thyself if thou wouldst rather be rich, or happy ; for to be rich is neither good in itself nor wholly in thy power, but to be happy is both good and possible."[1]

"It is better to be healthy on a narrow bed than sick in a wide one ; and so it is better to be contented with few possessions than have many and be discontented."[2]

"It is not poverty, but covetousness, that causes sorrow. It is not wealth, but philosophy, that gives security."[3]

"Make your daily food, not of expense and trouble, but of frugality and joy."[4]

"Time delivers fools from grief, and reason wise men."[5]

"He is wise who rejoices in what he has, and does not grieve for what he has not."[6]

"Fortify thyself in contentment, for this is a fortress which cannot be taken easily."[7]

"This is the height of piety, to know that the gods rule all things justly and well, and

---

[1] *Epictetus' Fragments*, xix (Didot); [2] *Frag.*, xxiv (Didot); [3] *Frag.*, xxv (Didot); [4] *Frag.*, xxix, in Didot, not in Higginson; [5] *Frag.*, cxxviii (Didot); [6] *Frag.*, cxxix (Didot); [7] *Frag.*, cxxxviii (Didot).

to resolve to submit to all that they do, and follow willingly their decree, since it is part of the best of plans." [1]

" Shall not our knowledge that God is our maker, father, and guardian, free us from grief or fear ?" [2]

" How easy to drive away every thought that is troublesome, or unfriendly, and be at peace at once." [3]

" Nothing comes upon any man which he is not formed to bear." [4]

" The mind turns every obstacle into an aid." [5]

" Nothing that happens injures me, unless I take it as an evil ; and it is in my power not to take it so." [6]

" Always remember that very little is needed for living a happy life." [7]

" Whatever happens is an opportunity for acting reasonably and kindly ; in short, becomingly, toward either God or man." [8]

[1] *Epictetus' Enchiridion,* chap. xxxi, sec. 1.   [2] *Discourses,* book i, chap. ix, sec. 7.

[3] *Marcus Aurelius' Meditations,* book v, sec. 2; [4] book v, sec. 18; [5] book v, sec 20; [6] book vii, sec. 14; [7] book vii, sec. 67; [8] book vii, sec. 68.

"Is it not better to use what thou hast, like a free man, than to long, like a slave, for what is not in thy power?"[1]

"Man becomes better and nobler by making a right use of all that comes to pass."[2]

"The soul has power to live most happily, if she will not be anxious about what is unimportant."[3]

COURAGE.

"O, Father, courage does not consist in fearing to live, but in resisting great evils, and not giving way; for to die on account of them is to be conquered."[4]

"She who can be compelled knows not how to die."[5]

"It is to make us noble, that God gives us such opportunities of growth in strength and courage as can be found only in adversity."[6]

[1] *Marcus Aurelius' Meditations*, book ix, sec. 40; [2] book x, sec. 33; [3] book xi, sec. 16.

[4] Speech of Antigone in the *Œdipidi Fragmento*, supposed to be by *Seneca*, line 190 [5] *Hercules Furens*, supposed to be by *Seneca*, line 426. [6] *Seneca's Dialogues*, book i, chap. iv, sec. 5.

"Calamity is opportunity for courage."[1]

"That courage is most to be relied on which reflects long, and moves slowly, and carries out what has been settled deliberately."[2]

"What is noble? A soul brave and steadfast under adversity; not only indifferent, but hostile, to dissipation—neither seeking nor flying danger; knowing how to make Fortune, instead of waiting for her; meeting all her changes calmly, and being never overcome either by her tempests or by her splendors."[3]

"It is better to grow braver than more learned, but neither can be done without the other."[4]

"Throw away all anxiety about life, and so make it pleasant."[5]

"A brave and wise man should not flee from life."[6]

"There is no happiness where there is any fear."[7]

[1] *Seneca's Dialogues*, book i, chap. iv, sec. 6; [2] book iii, chap. xi, sec. 8. [3] *Naturalium Quæstionum*, book iii, præf., sec 13, [4] book vi, chap. xxxii, sec. 1. [5] *Epistles*, iv, sec. 6; [6] *Ep.* xxiv, sec. 25, [7] *Ep.* lxxiv, sec. 5.

"True courage will avoid danger, but not fear it."[1]

"Courage is careful to preserve itself, and ready to endure what is evil in appearance only."[2]

"Life is warfare, and those who climb up and down steep paths, and go through dangerous enterprises, are the brave men and leaders in the camp; but to rest basely, at the cost of òthers' labors, is to be a coward, safe because despised."[3]

"Nothing is baser than to wish for death."[4]

"It is foolish to fear what cannot be escaped."[5]

> "In war, in dangers, oft, it has been known
> That fear has driven the headlong coward on.
> Give me the man whose cooler soul can wait
> With patience for the proper hour of fate!"[6]

"Toils and hardships exert no considerable power against any one who receives them with a contemptuous indifference, and reso-

---

[1] *Seneca's Epistles*, lxxxv, sec. 26; [2] *Ep* lxxxv, sec. 28; [3] *Ep*. xcvi, sec. 5; [4] *Ep*. cvii, sec. 22. [5] *De Remediis*, chap. i, sec. 3.

[6] *Lucan's Pharsalia*, book vii, line 104 in the original, and 164 in Rowe's version.

lutely closes with them, but they become much greater and more terrible to every adversary who retreats."[1]

"When you do what you have made up your mind is right, do not shrink from being seen by others, though they would all misunderstand you. If the act be wrong, fear to do it; but if it be right, why fear those who would be wrong in blaming it?"[2]

"Receive what is in your own power with courage; and what is not, with caution."[3]

"Be like a headland, standing firm against the waves that beat against it continually, and calming the raging sea."[4]

FORBEARANCE.

"The wise man will not punish offenders for his own revenge, but for their amendment."[5]

"He will treat them as the doctor does

---

[1] *Dion Chrysostom's Diogenes de Virtute*, vol. i, p. 147.

[2] *Epictetus' Enchiridion*, chap. xxxv, sec. 1.   [3] *Discourses*, book ii, chap. 1, sec. 6.

[4] *Marcus Aurelius' Meditations*, book iv, sec. 49.

[5] *Seneca's Dialogues*, book ii, chap. xii, sec. 3.

his patients; and what physician is angry with a maniac?"[1]

"That man is never safe who can be moved by injury or abuse."[2]

"The passions are as bad servants as leaders."[3]

"Reason never neeas the help of violent and reckless impulses over which she has no authority."[4]

"To be angry, even for those dear to us, is the sign, not of a noble soul, but of a weak one."[5]

"If there were reason for beginning to be angry, there would be none for ever ceasing to be."[6]

"In order not to be angry with anybody, you should pardon everybody. Your forgiveness is due to your race."[7]

"The soul which is incapable of anger may be not feeble, but possessed of stronger impulses."[8]

[1] *Seneca's Dialogues*, book ii, chap. xiii, sec. 1; [2] book ii, chap. xiii, sec. 5; [3] book iii, chap. ix, sec. 4; [4] book iii, chap. x, sec. 1; [5] book iii, chap. xii, sec. 5; [6] book iv, chap. ix, sec. 1; [7] book iv, chap. x, sec. 2; [8] book iv, chap. xvii, sec. 2.

"He who knows that men are not born wise, but have to become so, will never be angry with the erring."[1]

"The philosopher will not be the enemy, but the teacher, of sinners."[2]

"Fight against the beginnings of evil; but anger begins with thinking that we are injured."[3]

"Never does the suspicious man lack evidence."[4]

"If you hear that others have spoken ill of you, consider whether you have not done the same, and about many people."[5]

"We hold other people's vices before our eyes, but our own behind our backs."[6]

"Nobody but a madman would be angry with brute beasts, which do not know that they are injuring us."[7]

"The best cure for anger is delay."[8]

"Has a good man injured you? Don't believe so. A bad one? Don't wonder at it.

---

[1] *Seneca's Dialogues*, book iv, chap x, sec. 6; [2] book iv, chap. 10, sec. 7; [3] book iv, chap. xxii, sec. 2; [4] book iv, chap. xxiv, sec. 2; [5] book iv, chap. xxviii, sec. 4; [6] book iv, chap. xxviii, sec. 8; [7] book iv, chap. xxvi, sec. 4; [8] book iv, chap. xxix, sec. 1.

Others will avenge you, and indeed his own sin has already done so." [1]

"Let us inflict punishment without anger, and because it is useful, not because revenge is sweet." [2]

"Punishment should have reference to the future, not the past; and nobody be harmed because he sins, but only that he may be kept from sinning." [3]

"Him who is provoked at you, attack with kindnesses, and his wrath will cease." [4]

"If the wrong-doer be weak, spare him; if he be strong, spare yourself." [5]

"If he be your friend, he has done what was not intended; if he be your enemy, what might have been foreseen." [6]

"How much better to heal an injury than to avenge it!" [7]

"What must the soul of the angry man be, when his face is so hideous?" [8]

---

[1] *Seneca's Dialogues*, book iv, chap. xxx, sec. 2; [2] book iv, chap. xxxiii, sec. 1; [3] book iv, chap. xxxi, sec. 8; [4] book iv, chap. xxxiv, sec. 5; [5] book v, chap. v, sec. 8; [6] book v, chap. xxiv, sec. 3; [7] book v, chap. xxvii, sec. 1; [8] book iv, chap. xxxv, sec. 4

"He will be on his guard against his anger who understands that it begins by injuring him first of all."[1]

"Here is an invader that should be met on the frontier."[2]

"Canst thou wish anything worse than death to thy enemy? Be at ease. He will die even if you keep quiet."[3]

"Let me be good-natured with my friends, and mild and easy with my enemies."[4]

"There is no virtue more honorable to man than this, or more truly honored."[5]

"The wise man will pardon much, and save many souls because they are capable of being healed."[6]

"He will blame fortune alone for others' sins."[7]

"It is madness to think that we fix an end to passions which we cannot control at their beginning."[8]

---

[1] *Seneca's Dialogues*, book v, chap. iv, sec. 4; [2] book iii, chap. viii, sec. 2; [3] book v, chap. xliii, sec. 3; [4] book vii, chap. xx, sec. 5. [5] *De Clementia*, book i, chap. iii, sec. 2; [6] book ii, chap. vii, sec. 4. [7] *Epistles*, lxxxi, sec. 25; [8] *Ep.* lxxxv, sec. 13.

"There is only one day's difference between the insane and the angry."[1]

"Sin is never to be overcome by sin."[2]

"Better leave crime unpunished than condemn the innocent."[3]

"Thrasea used to say, 'He who hates vice hates mankind.'"[4]

"He is best and purest who pardons others as if he sinned himself daily, but avoids sinning as if he never pardoned."[5]

"Do not make an idol of your clothes, and you will not be angry at the thief."[6]

"The Cynic loves those who beat him, and is a father and brother toward all men."[7]

"He who is good and wise never quarrels with anybody, but tries to keep others out of strife."[8]

"Men exist for one another; therefore teach them or bear with them."[9]

---

[1] *Seneca's De Moribus,* sec. 106; [2] sec. 139.

[3] *Trajan,* in *Champigny's Les Antonins,* vol. 1, p. 423.

[4] *Pliny's Epistles,* xxii, book viii, sec. 3; [5] *Ep.* xxii, book viii, sec. 2.

[6] *Epictetus' Discourses,* book i, chap. xviii, sec. 11; [7] book iii, chap. xxii, sec. 54; [8] book iv, chap. v, sec. 1.

[9] *Marcus Aurelius' Meditations,* book ii, sec. 16.

"Does any one sin against thee? He has sinned against himself."[1]

"Do not think like him who wrongs thee, or as he would have thee, but see what is required by the truth."[2]

"How cruel it is not to allow men to seek for what they think proper and beneficial. But this, in some measure, thou dost in being angry at their misdeeds. Truly they are seeking after what is useful to them. Are they mistaken? Teach them so, but don't be angry."[3]

"Beware of feeling toward the cruel as they do toward others."[4]

"When thou art vexed at anything, thou hast forgotten that all events take place according to the laws of the universe; that close is the kinship of every man to the race, in fellowship, not of blood or birth, but of thought; that each mind flows forth out of God; and that each of us lives only for the moment, and loses only this."[5]

---

[1] *Marcus Aurelius' Meditations*, book iv, sec. 26; [2] book iv, sec. 11; [3] book vi, sec. 27; [4] book vii, sec. 65; [5] book xii, sec. 26.

"First, that we are made for each other.
Second, that we form our principles neces-
sarily, and are proud of our own actions.
Third, that when we do wrong, it is ignorantly and unwillingly—no soul being willingly
deprived of the truth, or of the power of acting justly, and the charge of injustice, ingratitude, avarice, or any other fault, always giving
pain. Fourth, that thou sinnest often thyself,
and are but a man like others, and what thou
dost abstain from, it is not so much from lack
of inclination as from cowardice or vanity.
Fifth, that thou dost not know when men do
wrong; since much is done from hidden motives, and one must have found out about
many things, to be able to judge another's
acts. Sixth, if much vexed or grieved, that
man's life is only for a moment, and we shall
all soon pass away. Seventh, that we are not
disturbed by others' actions, but by our own
opinions of them, and these opinions we can
change, by remembering that there comes no
shame upon us, except from our own sins.
Eighth, that our anger and regret at others'
acts cause us much more pain than do these

acts· in themselves. Ninth, that kindness is unconquerable, if it be only sincere ; for what will even the worst of men do to thee, if thou continue kind to him, and admonish him gently and in private?

"Remember these nine principles, as if given thee by the Muses, and thus begin to be a man. For mildness and gentleness are manlier and nobler, and show greater strength than anger, which is weakness.

"And if thou wilt, here is still a tenth gift, and from the master of the Muses: It were folly to expect the wicked not to sin, or not to treat thee as they do others."[1]

TEMPERANCE.

"Most people seek in the tavern for that pleasure which is to be found in labor."[2]

"To those who, to excuse their prodigality, urged that they spent only money that they did not know how to use otherwise, Zeno said, 'Would you forgive the cook who made his sauce too salt for you, and said it

[1] *Marcus Aurelius' Meditations*, book xi, sec. 18.
[2] *Zeno*, quoted in *Stobæus' Florilegium*, vol. i, p. 150.

was because he had more salt than he knew what to do with?'"[1]

"The ambassadors of King Antigonus invited Zeno to supper with other philosophers, who, as they drank, boasted of their learning, but he kept silence. And when the ambassadors asked him what they should report about him to their king, he replied, 'What you see; for the thing hardest to control of all is speech.'"[2]

"That pleasure which is worthy of a man consists in not overloading the body, nor exciting those passions whose rest is our safety."[3]

"Hunger needs little, but pride needs much."[4]

"It is best to keep the feasts of the people without their excesses."[5]

"The pleasures which the body gives are fleeting, soon regretted, and likely to become painful, unless restrained strictly.[6]

"True pleasure can never cease, nor be turned into pain."[7]

---

[1] *Stobæus' Florilegium*, vol. i, p. 271; [2] vol. ii, p. 33.
[3] *Seneca's De Beneficiis*, book vii, chap. ii, sec. 3. [4] *Epistles*, xvii, sec. 4; [5] *Ep.* xviii, sec. 4; [6] *Ep.* xxiii, sec. 6; [7] *Ep.* lix, sec. 2.

"Temperance reigns over the pleasures, hating and banishing some, moderating and regulating others, but always as means, not ends."[1]

"Think of pleasures in excess as punishments."[2]

"Nothing so favors temperance in all things as the thought how short and uncertain life is."[3]

"We should not expose our feeble souls to wine, beauty, or flattery."[4]

"What philosophers labor to teach in many volumes I can give you in a few words: Persevere, when healthy, in what you resolve upon when sick."[5]

PURITY.

"We must conquer our passions, not by strategy, but by main force; not by slight wounds, but by a deadly charge."[6]

---

[1] *Seneca's Epistles*, lxxxviii, sec. 29; [2] *Ep.* lxxxiii, sec. 27; [3] *Ep.* cxiv, sec. 27; [4] *Ep.* cxvi, sec. 6.

[5] *Pliny's Epistles*, xxvi, book vii, sec. 4.

[6] *Fabianus Papirius*, quoted in *Seneca's Dialogues*, book x, chap. x, sec. 1.

"We may think ourselves free from lust when we ask God for nothing which we cannot pray for openly."[1]

"So live among men as if God saw you, So speak to God as if men heard you."[2]

"What a wretched slavery he undergoes who is domineered over alternately by pleasure and pain, the most capricious and outrageous of tyrants."[3]

"Profligacy loses basely what she must recover in ways still more base."[4]

"Despising death, welcoming poverty, and restraining lust, these three give great delight."[5]

"We come into fortune's power, when we think anything but virtue good."[6]

"Pure, not only from forbidden pleasures, but from useless ones."[7]

"Often it is easier to renounce utterly than to enjoy moderately."[8]

---

[1] *Athenodorus*, quoted in *Seneca's Epistles*, sec. 5. [2] *Ep.*, sec. 5. [3] *Dialogues*, book vii, chap. iv, sec. 4. [4] *Naturalium Quæstionum*, book i, præf., sec. 6. [5] *Ep.* xxiii, sec. 4; [6] *Ep.* lxxiv, sec. 1; [7] *Ep.* cviii, sec. 14; [8] *Ep.* cviii, sec. 16.

"It is easy to keep base desires from entering, but hard to drive them out." [1]

"To restrain lust in its beginning, think about its end." [2]

"He who dies for love of wealth and pleasure shows that he never had a right to live." [3]

"Chastity, whose loss is every virtue's ruin." [4]

> "When thou canst truly call these virtues thine,
> Be wise and free, by Heaven's consent and mine;
> But if thy passions lord it in thy breast,
> Art thou not still a slave and still oppressed." [5]

"Don't be carried away by the fancy of any pleasure, but take time to reflect on how you may regret having indulged in it, and rejoice at having abstained." [6]

"Before thy marriage, keep thyself pure with all thy might." [7]

"The height of purity or impurity is in the soul." [8]

[1] *Seneca's Epistles,* cxvi, sec. 3.   [2] *De Moribus,* sec. 66; [3] sec. 119.   [4] *Fragments,* xiii, *De Matrimonio,* sec. 78.

[5] *Persius' Fifth Satire,* lines 113-14 and 128-30 in the original, and 217-18 and 236-37 in Dryden's version.

[6] *Epictetus' Enchiridion,* chap. xxxiv; [7] chap. xxxiii, sec. 8. [8] *Discourses,* book iv, chap. xi, sec. 5.

"Chastise your passions, that you may not be punished by them." [1]

"Wise men resist pleasures; fools are enslaved." [2]

"My mother taught me to keep myself not only from doing wrong, but even from imagining it." [3]

"The mind that is free from passion is a castle, and man has none more strong." [4]

"He who follows after pleasure will not keep himself from injustice." [5]

"Look at the courses of the stars, like one borne around with them; and think of the changes into each other of the elements. Such thoughts purify us of the filth of this earthly life." [6]

SELF-RESPECT.

"Those gifts of fortune which produce neither courage nor nobleness of soul, but insolence and baseness, should not be thought good, but bad." [7]

---

[1] *Epictetus' Fragments,* v, in Didot; [2] *Frag.*, cxi, in Didot.
[3] *Marcus Aurelius' Meditations,* book i, sec. 3; [4] book viii, sec. 48; [5] book ix, sec. 1; [6] book vii, sec. 47.
[7] *Posidonius,* quoted in *Denis' Histoire des Theories Morales,* vol. i, p. 282.

"Athenodorus said that he would not even take supper at the invitation of a man who would not feel obliged to him for doing so."[1]

"He who seeks true glory wishes not so much to be praised by voices as by hearts."[2]

"He who boasts his birth prides himself on what belongs to others."[3]

"Neither self-respect nor prudence is shown by him who readily thinks himself despised."[4]

"Satisfy conscience and do not work for reputation, but let this make itself, though it be worse than we deserve."[5]

"A man should neither be corrupted by externals nor conquered by them, but should value himself, and be confident in mind, prepared for any fortune, and the creator of his own life. His confidence should not be without knowledge, nor his knowledge without firmness."[6]

"Trust in yourself, and believe that you are walking in the right way."[7]

[1] *Seneca's Dialogues*, book ix, chap. vii, sec. 2. [2] *Thyestes*, supposed to be by Seneca, line 109. [3] *Hercules Furens*, supposed to be by Seneca, line 340. [4] *Dial.*, book ii, chap. x, sec. 3; [5] book v, chap. xli, sec. 2; [6] book vii, chap. viii, sec. 3; [7] book ix, chap. ii, sec. 2.

"Better be despised for candor, than tortured perpetually by attempts to deceive."[1]

"No one can be despised by others, unless he has first been despised by himself."[2]

"Nothing costs more than what is begged."[3]

"What you would be ashamed of feeling under obligation for do not accept."[4]

"No one is more ready to tread others under his feet than he who has become used to taking insults."[5]

"He who despises accidents, and is above vain desires, because all his riches are in himself; who knows that little is to be dreaded from man and nothing from God; who thinks every way easy along which virtue calls, and feels himself created for others' good; and who opens his conscience to the gods, and fears himself more than any one else—he stands safe and calm amid tempests; he has finished the most useful education."[6]

"So live as to have no secrets which you would not have known to your enemies."[7]

[1] *Seneca's Dialogues*, book ix, chap. xvii, sec. 2; [2] book xii, chap. xiii, sec. 6. [3] *De Beneficiis*, book ii, chap. i, sec. 4; [4] book ii, chap. xxiii, sec. 2; [5] book iii, chap. xxviii, sec. 6; [6] book vii, chap. i, sec. 3. [7] *Epistles*, iii, sec. 3.

"Instead of asking Fortune for her gifts, ask thyself not to ask for them."[1]

"What is wisdom? Always to wish for the same things."[2]

"When you have advanced far enough to reverence yourself, you may dismiss all mentors."[3]

"If thy deeds be noble, let all men know them; if they be base, what matters it that no one else knows them, since they are known to thee?"[4]

"What disgraces philosophy more than seeking applause?"[5]

"No one loves Virtue better than he who is willing to lose the credit rather than the consciousness of possessing her."[6]

"He labors not for virtue, but for glory, who would have his virtue known."[7]

"I had rather show you my feelings than speak them."[8]

"Fear thyself more than any other wit-

---

[1] *Seneca's Epistles*, xv, sec. 12; [2] *Ep.* xx, sec. 5; [3] *Ep.* xxv, sec. 6; [4] *Ep.* xlv, sec. 5; [5] *Ep.* liii, sec. 9; [6] *Ep.* lxxxi, sec. 20; [7] *Ep.* cxiii, sec. 32; [8] *Ep.* lxxv, sec, 2.

ness of thy sins, for thou art the only one thou canst never escape." [1]

"One of the causes of our unhappiness is that we live according to other people's examples, and are guided, not by reason, but by custom." [2]

"Glory should not be pursued by us, but follow us." [3]

"Experience has taught me not to ask advice when I have made up my mind what to do." [4]

"Rightly was Agrippinus held in honor, because, though worthy of the greatest praise, he never gave any to himself, but when he received any, blushed." [5]

"He who would be independent must seek for nothing and flee from nothing which depends on others." [6]

"Do not be troubled by such thoughts as, 'I shall live unhonored, and be nobody any-

[1] *Seneca's De Moribus,* sec. 59. [2] *Epistles,* cxxiii, sec. 6.

[3] *Pliny's Epistles,* viii, book i, sec. 14; [4] *Ep.* xiii, book ix, sec. 6.

[6] *Epictetus,* in *Stobæus' Florilegium,* vol. i, p. 164. [6] *Enchiridion,* chap. xiv, sec. 2.

where.' No evil or disgrace can befall thee through others, even if this be any. And is it your true work to get offices, or invitations to feasts?"[1]

"Never call yourself a philosopher, nor talk much about philosophy to those ignorant of it, but practice it. For instance, do not tell at meals how it is proper to eat, but eat as is proper."[2]

"He who believes that we are all born of God can never think of himself meanly or basely."[3]

"If you were the Jove or Minerva of Phidias, you would take care not to dishonor yourself and your maker; and now that Jove himself has made you, do you not care how you appear?"[4]

"We are created to be independent, modest, and noble of soul."[5]

"Do you wish to be useful, or to be praised?"[6]

---

[1] *Epictetus' Enchiridion,* chap. xxiv, sec. 1 ; [2] chap. xlvi, sec 1. [3] *Discourses,* book i, chap. iii, sec. 1; [4] book ii, chap. viii, secs. 18 and 19; [5] book iii, chap. vii, sec. 27; [6] book iii, chap. xxiii, sec. 7.

"The good and noble man does nothing for the sake of appearances, but everything for the sake of acting well."[1]

"Say boldly that he who flatters others is not free; and call him who does so for little things a little slave, and him who does it for great things a great one."[2]

"No one is owner of another's will."[3]

"Do not so much fear being disgraced by public opinion as by the truth."[4]

"The bounty of the gods placed me under a prince and father, who freed me from all pride, and taught me that it is possible to live in a palace and not want guards, or fine clothes, or torches, or statues, or any other ornaments; but imitate the habits of a private citizen, without lowering one's self, or neglecting what should be done by a ruler for the state."[5]

"A man should stand upright, and not be kept upright by others."[6]

[1] *Epictetus' Discourses*, book iii, chap. xxiv, sec. 50; [2] book iv, chap. i, sec. 55; [3] book iv, chap, xii, sec. 7. [4] *Fragments*, vi, in Didot.

[5] *Marcus Aurelius' Meditations*, book i, sec. 17; [6] book iii, sec. 5.

"How much trouble he escapes who does not look at what his neighbor says, or does, but at his own actions, to see that they be just and holy."[1]

"He is poor who has need of others, and has not in himself all he wants."[2]

"Do not make thyself either the tyrant or the slave of any man."[3]

"The man who has done a good deed makes no noise about it, but goes on to another, as the vine does to bear grapes again in their season."[4]

"I do my duty; other things trouble me not."[5]

"Take heed not to become like the Cæsars, but keep thyself pure, simple and dignified, a friend of justice and an enemy of pomp."[6]

"Simple and modest is the work of philosophy; may I not be tempted into pride!"[7]

"The pride of not being proud is the most hard to bear."[8]

[1] *Marcus Aurelius' Meditations,* book iv, sec. 18; [2] book iv, sec. 29; [3] book iv, sec. 31; [4] book iv, sec. 6; [5] book vi, sec. 22; [6] book vi, sec. 30; [7] book ix, sec. 29; [8] book xii, sec. 27.

"'*Even in a palace, life may be led well*' :
So spoke the inspired sage, purest of men,
Marcus Aurelius. . . .

    On his truth sincere
Who spoke these words, no shadow ever came
And when my ill-school'd spirit is aflame
Some nobler, ampler stage of life to win,
I'll stop and say, 'There were no succor here!
The aids to noble life are all within.'"[1]

[1] *Matthew Arnold's Dramatic and Lyric Poems*, p. 122, quoting the *Meditations*, book v sec. 16.

CHAPTER IV.

MAXIMS OF SELF-CULTURE.

NEXT will be given the maxims of Self-Culture, which here includes Diligence in general, and also growth in Health, Wealth, Wisdom, Friendship and Virtue. (The exhortations to reverence have been already given : see chapter ii, page 76.)

DILIGENCE.

"Employ life faithfully, and it is long enough for the grandest deeds; it is not the creator, but we ourselves that make it short; we are not paupers, but prodigals."[1]

"We live for but a small part of the time,

---

[1] *Seneca's Dialogues*, book x, chap. 1, secs. 3 and 4.

and the remaining part is not to be called life."[1]

"Nobody would give away his property to all comers, as everybody gives away his life."[2]

"He has the longest of lives who suffers no time to be lost."[3]

"He who lays out each day as if it were a life will neither fear nor long for the morrow."[4]

"The greatest waste of time is the delay which takes away our present, while promising a future."[5]

"Only to the busy belongs the present."[6]

"Labor nourishes noble souls."[7]

"It is a little thing not to refuse work; demand it."[8]

"It is our inconstancy, in beginning one thing after another, that makes life short."[9]

"They who do not keep striving to advance fall back; no one finds his progress as he left it."[10]

---

[1] *Seneca's Dialogues*, book x, chap. ii, sec. 2; [2] book x, chap. iii, sec. 1; [3] book x, chap. vii, sec. 5; [4] book x, chap. vii, sec. 9; [5] book x, chap. ix, sec 1; [6] book x, chap. x, sec. 6. [7] *Epistles*, xxxi, sec 4; [8] *Ep.* xxxi, sec. 6; [9] *Ep.* xxxii, sec. 2; [10] *Ep.* lxxi, sec. 35.

"We all have leisure for what we wish to do."[1]

"Think of each day as in itself a life."[2]

"A man of a nature truly generous looks upon labors as his principal antagonists, and loves to maintain with them an incessant contest by night and by day."[3]

"Never be careless, even about what is called unimportant."[4]

"If unwilling to rise in the morning, say to thyself, 'I awake to do the work of a man.'"[5]

"I was taught to endure labor, to want little, and to do things myself."[6]

HEALTH.

"Walk in the country, so that thy mind may expand and exalt itself in the fresh air and free sky. Its power and keenness increase during repose, and it should not be

---

[1] *Seneca's Epistles*, cvi, sec. 1; [2] *Ep.* ci, sec. 10.

[3] *Dion Chrysostom's Diogenes de Virtute*, vol. i, p. 146.

[4] *Epictetus' Discourses*, book ii, chap. vi, sec. 2.

[5] *Marcus Aurelius' Meditations*, book v, sec. 1; [6] book i, sec. 5.

kept always strained, but be directed sometimes to amusements."[1]

"Our duty is to follow nature, but it is contrary to nature to torture one's body, to dislike cleanliness and seek filth, or to make use of rough and dirty food. Philosophy requires frugality, but not self-torment."[2]

"Follow this sound and safe rule of life—to indulge the body just so much as its health requires."[3]

"I acknowledge that it should be cared for and favored, but I deny that it should be served, for he who serves it serves many masters."[4]

"I would not have you always poring over books and tablets. Let the mind have time, not indeed to be weakened, but to be refreshed."[5]

"We need amusements, but there should be some work in them, that even from them we may get good."[6]

---

[1] *Seneca's Dialogues,* book ix, chap. xvii, secs. 5, 6 and 8.
[2] *Epistles,* v, secs. 4 and 5; [3] *Ep.* viii, sec. 5; [4] *Ep.* xiv, sec. 1;
[5] *Ep.* xv, sec. 6; [6] *Ep.* lviii, sec. 25.

"A stomach which can wait patiently, and endure rough treatment, is an important condition of liberty."[1]

"It is wonderful how much the mind is excited by moving the body."[2]

WEALTH.

"They are mad, who make no account of riches, health, freedom from pain, and integrity of the body, nor take any care to attain them."[3]

"The wise man will not love wealth, but yet he will prefer to have it. He will receive it into his house, though not into his heart, not rejecting it, but controlling it, and willing to have larger opportunities for virtue."[4]

"In poverty there can be no virtues but perseverance and self-respect, but wealth gives a free field for temperance, generosity, economy, industry, and magnanimity."[5]

[1] *Seneca's Epistles,* cxxiu, sec. 3.

[2] *Pliny's Epistles,* vi, book i, sec. 2.

[3] *Chrysippus,* quoted in *Plutarch's Morals,* Goodwin's Ed., vol. iv, p. 437.

[4] *Seneca's Dialogues,* book vii, chap. xxi, sec. 4; [5] book vii, chap. xxii, sec. 1.

"Cease, then, to forbid philosophers to have money. Wisdom has never been condemned to poverty. The wise man may have great riches, but none which have been gained by disgracing himself or wronging others, or which have been stained with blood. He will not reject the bounty of fortune, nor will he blush for what he has gained honestly, though he will not glory in it. He will not let a penny cross his threshold if it comes wickedly, but he will not disown the wealth, however great, which is given by fortune, or earned by his own virtues, nor will he shut it out."[1]

"I deny that riches are good in themselves, but I confess that they are worth having and useful, and may be of great help in life."[2]

"Money is the fool's master, but the wise man's slave."[3]

"Among useful things is money, not in superfluity, but in quantity sufficient for all moderate desires."[4]

[1] *Seneca's Dialogues*, book vii, chap. xxiii, secs. 1, 2 and 3; [2] book vii, chap. xxiv, sec. 5; [3] book vii, chap. xxvi, sec. 1. [4] *De Beneficiis*, book i, chap. xi, sec. 5.

"He is great, who uses earthenware as if it were silver, nor is he less noble who uses the silver as if it were earthenware. He has a weak soul who cannot bear wealth."[1]

"He alone is worthy to be a god who has looked down upon riches. Not that I would forbid them to you, but that I would have you possess them fearlessly."[2]

WISDOM.

"Zeno said to one who was more desirous to talk than to listen: 'Young man, Nature has given us two ears, and but one tongue, in order that we may hear twice as much as we speak.'"[3]

"Zeno compared the arts of the logician to accurate measures, used to measure out, not wheat or anything else useful, but only dung and chaff."[4]

"Zeno said that we are not so poor in anything as in time, for life is short and art is long, especially that of healing the diseases of the mind."[5]

[1] *Seneca's Epistles*, v, sec. 6; [2] *Ep.* xviii, sec. 13.
[3] *Stobæus' Florilegium*, vol. ii, p. 39; [4] vol. iii, p. 116; [5] vol. iii, p. 233.

"To adopt the good advice of another seemed to Zeno a proof of greater virtue than originally to conceive what is just and right."[1]

"One day does more for the educated man than the longest life for the untaught."[2]

"From early youth we can give ourselves to looking at the truth, finding a rule of life, and obeying it quietly."[3]

"He who studies the universe serves God."[4]

"Nature, conscious of her own wisdom and beauty, has created us as observers of lofty spectacles."[5]

"Such are the researches for which we are born, that we should find all the time allotted us short."[6]

"Many would reach wisdom, did they not suppose they had already arrived there."[7]

"The mind of man is by nature active and ready to move, so that it finds all opportu-

---

[1] *Julian's Works,* vol. i, p. 39.

[2] *Posidonius,* quoted in *Seneca's Epistles,* lxxviii, sec. 28.

[3] *Seneca's Dialogues,* book viii, chap. ii, sec. 1; [4] book viii, chap. iv, sec. 2; [5] book viii, chap. v, sec. 3; [6] book viii, chap. v, sec. 7; [7] book ix, chap. i, sec. 16.

nities of exciting and elevating itself precious."[1]

"The mind can reach nothing grand and difficult, unless it passes out of the beaten track into regions where it has feared to go."[2]

"Those alone have leisure who devote themselves to wisdom; they alone live, for they enjoy not only their own years, but all the ages."[3]

"We are discharging true duties when we make friends with Zeno, Pythagoras, Aristotle and the other masters of noble callings. None of them lacks leisure for his visitors, fails to send them away happier and more attached to him, or lets them go back empty-handed."[4]

"We often say that we could not choose our parents, yet there are many families of most noble souls, any one of which is ready to adopt us, as an heir, not only of the name, but of the wealth. They will open for us the way to immortality."[5]

---

[1] *Seneca's Dialogues,* book ix, chap. ii, sec. 11; [2] book ix, chap. xvii, sec. 11; [3] book x, chap. xiv, sec. 1; [4] book x, chap. xiv, sec. 5; [5] book x, chap. xv, sec. 3.

"This grand and noble world, and this mind which beholds it with admiration, and is its noblest part—these belong to us, and will continue with us."[1]

"It is our minds that make us rich."[2]

"I would lead you where all seek refuge who flee from fortune, to those noble studies which will heal thy wounds, and take away all thy sorrow: they will console and delight you; and if they really possess your soul, they will leave no room for sorrow or anxiety to enter in."[3]

"As the tools we handle daily are kept free from rust and dirt, so what we think of often never slips from the memory."[4]

"There is no fickleness in forsaking an error which has been exposed, and saying openly, 'I thought otherwise, but I was mistaken.' It is folly to say, 'What I have said

[1] *Seneca's Dialogues*, book xii, chap. viii, sec. 4; [2] book xii, chap. xi, sec. 5; [3] book xii, chap. xvii, secs. 3 and 5. (It should be observed that this language is addressed by Seneca to his mother, Helvia. Her earlier studies had been restricted by his father, for which he expresses much regret in the passage partly quoted.) [4] *De Beneficiis* book iii, chap. ii, sec. 3.

must remain fixed.' There is no disgrace in having our opinions change with the circumstances."[1]

"How much better worth our while to know what we should do, than what has been already done!"[2]

"What will be the reward of our studies? The noblest that could be wished: the knowledge of nature."[3]

"Strength of mind can come in no other way than by studying diligently and observing nature [A contemplatione naturæ]."[4]

"Beware of your habit of reading many authors and all kinds of books, lest this be a sign of frivolity and indecision. Always read books of acknowledged worth, and if you get diverted to others, return ever to these."[5]

"It is laboring, and yet doing nothing, to follow literary plans which have no effect if kept to ourselves, and if published make us appear, not learned, but tiresome."[6]

[1] *Seneca's De Beneficiis*, book iv, chap. xxxviii, sec. 1.   [2] *Naturalium Quæstionum*, book iii, præf., sec. 7; [3] book vi, chap. iv, sec. 2; [4] book vi, chap. xxxii, sec. 1.   [5] *Epistles*, ii, secs. 2-4. [6] *Dialogues*, book x, chap. xiii. sec. 1.

"You remember the delight of throwing aside the boy's clothes, and putting on the manly toga. Expect yet more joy from putting off a childish mind, and being enrolled by philosophy as a man."[1]

"Do not fear that you have wasted your study if you have taught yourself."[2]

"Memory guards what is entrusted to us, but knowledge consists in making it our own, and not thinking of masters. If we are satisfied with what has been found out, we shall find nothing more. They who have gone before us are not our masters, but our guides Truth is open to all, and has not yet been taken possession of, but many discoveries will be left for future ages."[3]

"Make our inherited wisdom grow as it passes on to later generations. Much will remain to be done by them, and something may be added by him who lives a thousand centuries hereafter."[4]

"Wouldst thou subject all things to thyself, subject thyself to wisdom."[5]

[1] *Seneca's Epistles*, iv, sec 2; [2] *Ep.* vii, sec. 9; [3] *Ep.* xxxiii, secs. 8, 10 and 11· [4] *Ep.* lxiv, sec. 7; [5] *Ep.* xxxvii.

"It matters not how many, but how good, books you have." [1]

"Eloquence harms those whom it leads to love itself and not its subjects." [2]

"Rise up, and leave behind you the literary play of those who turn the greatness of philosophy into syllables, and make it appear not grand, but difficult." [3]

"The soul is in chains, until philosophy cheers her with the knowledge of nature, and lets her mount from what is earthy to the divine." [4]

"Love wisdom, and this love will arm you against the strongest foes." [5]

"No one drives away vice, until in its place he accepts wisdom." [6]

"Ease without letters is a living death and burial." [7]

"The arts serve life, but wisdom rules it." [8]

"Study not to know more, but better." [9]

---

[1] *Seneca's Epistles*, xlv, sec. 1; [2] *Ep.* lii, sec. 14; [3] *Ep.* lxxi, sec. 6; [4] *Ep.* lxv, sec. 16; [5] *Ep.* lxxiv, sec. 21; [6] *Ep* lxxv, sec. 10; [7] *Ep.* lxxxii, sec. 3; [8] *Ep.* lxxxv, sec. 33; [9] *Ep.* lxxxix, sec. 23.

"In the perfection of our reason lies all the happiness of life."[1]

"I must keep reading, in order to keep dissatisfied with myself."[2]

"Let us imitate the bees, and put into definite order what we get from reading widely, taking care to digest it well enough to have it reach the mind, and not merely the memory."[3]

"Read much, but not many books."[4]

"Only the educated are free."[5]

"Mind, knowledge, right reason—here seek the essence of goodness."[6]

"What is the first business of him who seeks wisdom? To cast away self-conceit."[7]

"Your excellence is your reason; adorn that and make it beautiful."[8]

"Every soul is created to accept what is true, reject what is false, and doubt what is uncertain."[9]

---

[1] *Seneca's Epistles,* xcii, sec. 2; [2] *Ep.* lxxxiv, sec. 1; [3] *Ep.* lxxxiv, secs. 5 and 7.

[4] *Pliny's Epistles,* ix, book vii, sec. 15.

[5] *Epictetus' Discourses,* book ii, chap. i, sec. 25; [6] book ii, chap. viii, secs. 2 and 3; [7] book ii, chap. xvii, sec. 1; [8] book iii, chap. i, sec. 26; [9] book iii, chap. iii, sec. 2.

"The duty of the philosopher is to protect, not his wine, his oil, or his body, but his reason."[1]

"Virtue unbinds the chain of the soul, by teaching, experience and exercise."[2]

"Let nothing be more precious to thee than the truth."[3]

"Take care rather to leave thy children well taught than rich; for the hope of the wise is better than the wealth of the ignorant."[4]

"He who cultivates wisdom cultivates the knowledge of God."[5]

"Never be contented with a superficial apprehension of anything."[6]

"By nothing is thy mind enlarged so much as by searching with method and fidelity into every event of life, and seeing what a universe this is, and what use everything therein serves, and what value it has for the great whole, as well as for man, the citizen of that

[1] *Epictetus' Discourses*, book III, chap. x, sec. 16. [2] *Fragments*, x (Didot); [3] *Frag.*, cxxxix (Didot); [4] *Frag.*, cxlv (Didot); [5] *Frag.*, cli (Didot)

[6] *Marcus Aurelius' Meditations*, book i, sec. 7.

highest city, in which all others are but houses." [1]

"Have these two rules ever before thine eyes : to do only what thy royal reason shows thee is useful to mankind ; and if any one can correct thy opinion, to change it, following not pleasure or glory, but philanthropy and justice." [2]

"As thou thinkest most often, so will be thy character ; for by the thoughts the soul is dyed." [3]

"A man's worth is that of those things about which he is busy." [4]

"Remember that to change thy mind, and follow him who sets thee right, does not lessen thy independence." [5]

"The name of Universal Nature is Truth. He who lies, or acts unjustly intentionally, is impious. And so is he who errs unintentionally, for he fights against Nature, from whom he has received the power, which he neglects, of telling the false from the true." [6]

[1] *Marcus Aurelius' Meditations*, book iii, 'sec. 11; [2] book iv, sec. 12; [3] book v, sec. 16; [4] book vii, sec. 3; [5] book viii, sec. 16; [6] book ix, sec. 1.

FRIENDSHIP.

"No one is so high in fortune as not to need a friend all the more, because he needs nothing else."[1]

"Before we form a friendship we should criticise, but after forming it we should only trust."[2]

"It is vicious either to trust nobody or to trust everybody."[3]

"Why should I seek a friend? That I may have some one I could die for. How should I enter into friendship? Not in hope of gain, or in fear of change of fortune."[4]

"Love sometimes harms, but friendship always helps."[5]

"I seek the society, not of those among whom chance or birth throws me, but of those in every age and land who are most virtuous."[6]

"Nothing does more to strengthen the character in virtue, and free it from vice, than the society of the good."[7]

[1] *Seneca's De Beneficiis*, book vi, chap. xxix, sec. 2. [2] *Epistles*, iii, sec. 2; [3] *Ep.* iii, sec. 4; [4] *Ep.* ix, secs. 10 and 12; [5] *Ep.* xxxv, sec. 1; [6] *Ep.* lxii, sec. 2; [7] *Ep.* xciv, sec. 40.

"A man cannot retain his wisdom, unless
he has friends like himself. The highest and
holiest ideas are best discussed in common,
and by combining various men's ideas. He
who cultivates others' virtue cultivates also
his own."[1]

"Consider not how many, but what sort
of, people you please."[2]

"Advise a friend in private; praise him
openly."[3]

Prosperity gives friends; adversity proves
them."[4]

"He who associates calmly with the wicked
is one of them himself."[5]

"No one will ever persuade me that I
love my friends too much."[6]

"Try to gather around your house, not
herds of oxen, but troops of friends."[7]

"Flee from the friendship of the wicked
and the hatred of the good."[8]

"Choose not the most pleasant, but the

---

[1] *Seneca's Epistles*, cix, secs. 9, 12 and 14. [2] *De Moribus*,
sec. 8; [3] sec. 12; [4] sec. 51, [5] sec. 75.

[6] *Pliny's Epistles*, xxviii, book vii, sec. 3.

[7] *Epictetus' Fragments*, xlvii (Didot); [8] *Frag.*, cliii (Didot).

most useful, of physicians and of friends."[1]

"How to receive favors from my friends without either feeling humbled or acting ungratefully, and that I should not disregard a friend who finds fault even unreasonably, but strive to restore him to his usual disposition—these were among my lessons from Apollonius and Catulus."[2]

"When thou wouldst be joyful, call to mind the good qualities of those who live with thee."[3]

"Do not be ashamed of being helped, for thou must do thy duty like a soldier storming a wall. What if thou art too lame to mount the battlement alone, but canst do it with another's help?"[4]

"He who is separate from any neighbor has fallen away from the whole community."[5]

VIRTUE.

"He who repents of his sins is already almost innocent."[6]

[1] *Epictetus' Fragments*, clvii (Didot).
[2] *Marcus Aurelius' Meditations*, book i, secs. 8 and 13;
[3] book vi, sec. 48; [4] book vii, sec. 7; [5] book xi, sec. 8.
[6] Chorus in *Agamemnon*, supposed to be by *Seneca*, line 243.

"No one can think himself free from vice, and if he call himself so he follows some other testimony than that of conscience."[1]

"The safest road to virtue is repentance."[2]

"Goodness consists mainly in wishing to become good."[3]

"He who can tell his dreams has awaked; and he who can tell his faults has repented."[4]

"Is it not plain that patience, courage, perseverance, and the other virtues which resist difficulties and conquer fortune, are to be gained only by effort and struggle?"[5]

"Search yourself, and see whether you are learning to philosophize, or to live by philosophy. Her work is not to dazzle the untaught, or to pass away the time, but to form and build up the soul, order the life, and rule the conduct, showing what should be done or left undone."[6]

"It is vain to hope that virtue will de-

[1] *Seneca's Dialogues*, book iii, chap. xiv, sec. 3. [2] *Naturalium Quæstionum*, book iii, præf, sec. 3. [3] *Epistles*, xxxiv, sec. 3; [4] *Ep.* liii, sec. 8. [5] *Dialogues*, book vii, chap. xxv, sec. 6. [6] *Ep.* xvi, sec. 3.

scend into our souls by chance. We must work for her, though in truth the labor need not be great, if we begin to form our character before it is hardened in vice. And even then it should not be despaired of."[1]

"We must learn virtue by unlearning vice. And virtue, when once gained, remains with us. and cannot be unlearned."[2]

"The noblest virtue is not fostered by incense and garlands, but by ~~sweat~~ and blood."[3]

"As weapons to chained hands, so are precepts to sinful souls."[4]

"Feeling is king when it seeks the right, but when it is unruly it takes a hateful name, and becomes tyrant."[5]

"Our nature has strength enough, if we are only willing to gather and use it all; we cannot plead lack of power, but only of intention."[6]

"It is our scorn for what can be had easily that makes all our life difficult."[7]

---

[1] *Seneca's Epistles*, l, sec. 5; [2] *Ep.* l, sec. 8; [3] *Ep.* lxvii, sec. 12; [4] *Ep.* xcv, sec. 38; [5] *Ep.* cxiv, sec. 24; [6] *Ep.* cxvi, sec. 8; [7] *Ep.* xc, sec. 18.

"Virtue is the only thing which does not change, so as to be sometimes good and sometimes bad."[1]

"What a paltry innocence to be as good as the law requires!"[2]

"The Stoic loves only virtue, and would not leave her to gain immortality."[3]

"She receives no sordid lover."[4]

"For her all things are to be endured."[5]

"She is self-satisfied and permanent, while vice is ever changing."[6]

"Only that by which the character is made better is good."[7]

"What is noble? To let no base purpose enter the soul; to lift pure hands to heaven; to seek nothing which can be gained only at another's loss; to pray for that about which there is no rivalry—a virtuous mind; and to think of everything else, however precious to others, however richly given to ourselves, as soon to pass away."[8]

[1] *Seneca's Epistles*, xcv, sec. 35. [2] *Dialogues*, book iv, chap. xxviii, sec. 2. [3] *Ep.* lxxxviii, sec. 5. [4] *De Beneficiis*, book iv, chap. xxiv, sec. 2. [5] *Ep.* lxxvi, sec. 26; [6] *Ep.* xlvii, sec. 21; [7] *Ep.* lxxvi, sec. 17. [8] *Naturalium Quæstionum*, book iii, præf., sec. 14.

"We have all one common origin, and no one is nobler than others, unless his disposition is more upright and ready for good deeds."[1]

"Who is nobly born? He who is by nature virtuous. It is the character that makes the noble."[2]

"Virtue is the same, whether she is reached through joys or griefs."[3]

"As the sun dims all lesser lights, so does she cause grief, trouble and injury to fade away."[4]

"She is sufficient by herself to complete the happiness of life."[5]

"What can he desire, who has every virtue?"[6]

"If reverence, fidelity, and prudence are preserved, the man is saved; but if either of these be lost, he also perishes."[7]

"Nothing great is produced suddenly, any more than is a grape or a fig. If you wish

---

[1] *Seneca's De Beneficiis*, book iii, chap. xxviii, sec. 1.
[2] *Epistles*, xliv, sec. 5; [3] *Ep.* lxvi, sec. 19; [4] *Ep.* lxvi, sec. 20;
[5] *Ep.* lxxxv, sec. 1; [6] *Ep.* xcii, sec. 4.

[7] *Epictetus' Discourses*, book i, chap. xxviii, sec. 21.

for figs, you must wait for the blossoming, the setting, and the ripening of the fruit ; then, since not even the fruit of a fig-tree becomes perfect suddenly, or in a single hour, do you expect to possess quickly and easily the ripe fruit of the human mind ?"[1]

"It is better sometimes to own that we sin, but usually to behave well, than seldom to confess our faults, but often commit them."[2]

"If you would beautify your city with votive offerings, first set up within yourself the most beautiful ones, namely : meekness, justice, and philanthropy."[3]

"You will do the most good to your city, not by raising the roofs, but by exalting the souls therein. It is better that great souls should dwell in little houses than that base slaves should make dens of spacious mansions."[4]

"Better die than live ill."[5]

"How few are the laws which we must

---

[1] *Epictetus' Discourses*, book i, chap. xv, secs. 7 and 8.
[2] *Fragments*, iv (Didot); [3] *Frag.*, lxxx (Didot); [4] *Frag.*, lxxxi (Didot); [5] *Frag.*, xcii (Didot).

master to live happily and like the gods, who require of us nothing more!"[1]

"What should we desire earnestly? Only this : just thoughts, philanthropic actions, words which never deceive, and readiness to accept whatever happens, as a necessary part of the great whole."[2]

"Show forth that which is wholly in thine own power—sincerity, dignity, industry, self-control, contentment with what is assigned thee, however little ; kindness, independence, magnanimity, and disregard of luxury or frivolity."[3]

"Good fortune is good intentions, good impulses, and good deeds."[4]

"If anything is possible for man, and peculiar to him, think that this can be attained by thee."[5]

"Look within : there is the fountain of good which will always gush forth, if thou wilt always dig."[6]

---

[1] *Marcus Aurelius' Meditations*, book ii, sec. 5; [2] book iv, sec. 33; [3] book v, sec. 5; [4] book v, sec. 36; [5] book vi, sec. 19; [6] book vii, sec. 59.

"Thou art suffering justly; for thou wishest to become good to-morrow, rather than to be so to-day."[1]

"Use the present thoughtfully and justly, for life is short."[2]

[1] *Marcus Aurelius' Meditations*, book viii, sec. 22; [2] book iv, sec. 26.

CHAPTER V.

MAXIMS OF BENEVOLENCE.

THE Stoic literature is peculiarly rich in exhortations to Benevolence, taking this virtue to include Toleration, Family Affection, Gratitude, Charity, Patriotism, and Philanthropy. Some of these precepts will be seen to be older than Christianity.

TOLERATION.

"As we bear with children, so the philosopher will bear with everybody." [1]

"Human life consists of kindness and har-

---

[1] *Seneca's Dialogues*, book ii, chap xii, sec. 1.

mony, and is held together for mutual help, not by terror, but by love."[1]

"The universe is holy, and so are all its parts. It is wrong to harm any man, for he is thy fellow-citizen in the greatest of cities. Nor can society be preserved without mutual love, and therefore men should spare each other."[2]

"What a monster is he who rages at his fellow-men!"[3]

"Let us honor humanity, and cause no danger or fear to any one."[4]

"As glory follows those who flee from her, so is gratitude given most richly to those who tolerate ingratitude."[5]

"We make others better by bearing with them, and worse by finding fault."[6]

"Take care not to be either like the bad because there are many of them, or hostile to the many because they are not like yourself."[7]

---

[1] *Seneca's Dialogues*, book iii, chap. v, sec. 3; [2] book iv, chap. xxxi, sec. 7; [3] book v, chap. iii, sec. 2; [4] book v, chap. xliii, sec. 5. [5] *De Beneficiis*, book v, chap. i, sec. 4; [6] book vii, chap. xxviii, sec. 3. [7] *Epistles*, vii, sec. 8.

"Let your philosophy make you quit your own vices, but not find fault with other people's, or shock public opinion, or act as if you condemn whatever you do not yourself do."[1]

"What compulsion does, passes away; what persuasion does, endures."[2]

"Euphrates attacked vices, not men, and did not scourge, but persuaded, the erring."[3]

"It is like an ignorant man to blame others for his misfortunes, like a beginner in philosophy to blame himself, and like one well taught to blame neither himself nor others."[4]

"Will you not bear with your brother, who has God for his ancestor and is of your own heavenly race?"[5]

"However my brother treats me, I must do my duty by him; that is all that need concern me."[6]

"The injury itself harms greatly the wrong-doer."[7]

[1] *Seneca's Epistles*, ciii, sec. 5. [2] *De Moribus*, sec. 110.
[3] *Pliny's Epistles*, x, book i, sec. 7.
[4] *Epictetus' Enchiridion*, chap. v. [5] *Discourses*, book i, chap. xiii, sec. 3; [6] book iii, chap. x, secs. 19 and 20; [7] book iv, chap. v, sec. 10.

"It is better to advise than to reproach."[1]

"Sextus taught me to bear with ignorant people, and those who make up their minds without examination."[2]

"If any one hurt us in gymnastic exercises, we do not treat him as an enemy, but we keep out of his way good-naturedly. Let us do the same everywhere else, overlooking much in those who encounter us, and not beating them, but only keeping out of their way."[3]

"If thou be able, teach others what is right; if thou be not, remember that meekness was given thee for this."[4]

"Be on thy guard against being driven either from thy right purposes by those who stand in thy way, or from thy kind feelings toward them. This also is deserting thy post, to be estranged from him who is by nature thy kinsman and friend."[5]

"The human soul dishonors herself whenever she separates herself so far from the uni-

---

[1] *Epictetus' Fragments,* cvii (Didot).

[2] *Marcus Aurelius' Meditations,* book i, sec. 9; [3] book vi, sec. 20; [4] book ix, sec. 11; [5] book xi, sec. 9.

verse as to be vexed at anything, or turns away from any man in anger."[1]

FAMILY AFFECTION.

"Never make it either necessary or profitable for your child to ask for anything abjectly."[2]

"This surely is a man's duty, to be useful, if he can, to many; if not, to a few; if that may not be, to those nearest him, or at least to himself; for as he makes himself capable of serving others, he serves the public good."[3]

"The wise man will be glad to marry and have children, for he had rather not live at all than live alone."[4]

"What is more pleasant than to be so dear to your wife as to be on this account dearer to yourself?"[5]

"As soon as a child is born to us, it is no longer in our power not to love it and care for it."[6]

[1] *Marcus Aurelius' Meditations*, book ii, sec. 16.

[2] *Seneca's Dialogues*, book iv, chap. xxi, sec. 4; [3] book viii, chap. iii, sec. 5. [4] *Epistles*, ix, sec. 17; [5] *Ep.* civ, sec. 5.

[6] *Epictetus' Discourses*, book i, chap. xxiii, sec. 5.

"Severus commanded me to love those who dwell with me."[1]

"Love practically the men with whom thy lot is cast."[2]

"To love our neighbor is a property which shows a soul endowed with reason."[3]

GRATITUDE.

"Should a gift not prove a benefit, it would yet be ungrateful not to return it, as if it were."[4]

"A kindness should be returned in the same spirit in which it is bestowed."[5]

"He who gives ought to forget it immediately, but he who receives never."[6]

"He who takes gratefully has paid the first installment of his debt."[7]

"We should be neither squeamish nor abject in taking favors."[8]

"The chief cause of our ingratitude is too

[1] *Marcus Aurelius' Meditations*, book i, sec. 14; [2] book vi, sec. 39; [3] book xi, sec. 1.

[4] *Cleanthes*, in *Seneca's De Beneficiis*, book v, chap. xiv, sec. 1. [5] *De Benef.*, book i, chap. i, sec. 8; [6] book ii, chap. x, sec. 4; [7] book ii, chap. xxii, sec. 1; [8] book ii, chap. xxiv, sec. 2.

high an opinion of ourselves. This makes us think that we deserve everything, so that we take a kindness as if it were our due, and never think ourselves treated well enough."[1]

"Gratitude returns intention for intention, as well as act for act."[2]

"He is most ungrateful who forgets what has been given him."[3]

"Remembering our benefactors needs no time, or skill, or opportunity, but only good intentions."[4]

"To forget a kindness proves that we have never kept it in our thoughts, or meant to be grateful."[5]

"It may happen that he who returns a favor is ungrateful, and he is grateful who does not."[6]

"The ingrate is pleased for the time, the grateful man for ever."[7]

"No other vice is so hostile to the harmony of the human race as ingratitude."[8]

---

[1] *Seneca's De Beneficiis*, book ii, chap. xxvi, sec. 1; [2] book ii, chap. xxxv, sec. 1; [3] book iii, chap. i, sec. 3; [4] book iii, chap. ii, sec. 2; [5] book iii, chap. ii, sec. 1; [6] book iii, chap. vii, sec. 6; [7] book iii, chap. xvii, sec. 3; [8] book iv, chap. xviii, sec. 1.

"He who repays a kindness because he hopes for another is ungrateful."[1]

"He who hurries to repay an obligation shows an unwillingness to remain under it—which is ingratitude."[2]

"No one who knows his obligations, and heartily wishes to discharge them, need think himself outdone in kindness."[3]

"I should be unjust, as well as ungrateful, if I were not glad to have him who benefits me benefit himself, also."[4]

"Do not wish that your benefactor may need to be repaid by you, but only that you may be able to repay him, if he needs it."[5]

"What is received should be repaid, however wicked the giver may become. Crime must be cured by justice, not by ingratitude. Do not let another's guilt make you sin."[6]

"He is an ingrate who repays a kindness without giving interest."[7]

"If I could not be grateful without seem-

[1] *Seneca's De Beneficiis*, book iv, chap. xx, sec. 3; [2] book iv, chap. xl, sec. 5; [3] book v, chap. iv, sec. 1; [4] book vi, chap. xiii, sec. 2; [5] book vi, chap. xxviii, sec. 3; [6] book vii, chap. xvii, sec. 2. [7] *Epistles*, lxxxi, sec. 18.

ing ungrateful, or repay my benefactor without appearing to injure him, I ought to carry out my noble purpose calmly through ill-report."[1]

CHARITY.

"To have kingdoms is fortune; to give them, virtue."[2]

"Why not take care of your short life, and make it pleasant for others, and also for yourself?"[3]

"If you would have other people feel grateful to you, you must not only help them, but love them."[4]

"It is base to be outdone in kindness."[5]

"Avarice denies to herself what she takes from others."[6]

"I measure my gifts, not by number or weight, but according to the worth of the receiver; never do I value highly what has been given to those who deserve it."[7]

[1] *Seneca's Epistles*, lxxxi, sec. 20. [2] Speech of Atreus, in the *Thyestes*, supposed to be by Seneca, line 529. [3] *Dialogues*, book v, chap. xliii, sec. 1. [4] *De Beneficiis*, book ii, chap. xi, sec. 5; [5] book v, chap. ii, sec. 1. [6] *Naturalium Quæstionum*, book i, præf., sec. 6. [7] *Dial.*, book vii, chap. xx, sec. 4.

"The wise man will help those who weep, but not imitate them. He will give his hand to the shipwrecked, hospitality to the exile, and aid to the poor; not proudly, like many, who wish to seem compassionate, yet who scorn those they help and fear to be approached by them, but like a man who helps his fellow-men on account of the universal brotherhood." [1]

"He will be, not pitiful, but helpful and useful, as one born for the common weal and the public good, of which he will give every one a share. Even those who are deservedly unfortunate he will try kindly to reform; though he will take more pleasure in helping those who suffer innocently, and in standing between them and adversity. What more noble use can be made of wealth and strength?" [2]

"No one is grateful for what he has extorted. We find many ingrates, and we make more." [3]

[1] *Seneca's De Clementia*, book ii, chap vi, sec. 2; [2] book ii, chap. vi, sec. 3. [3] *De Beneficiis*, book i, chap. i, secs. 4 and 7.

"If your kindness be returned, there is gain ; if it be not, there is no loss."[1]

"Kindness is always good. It is the intention which endears what is cheap, ennobles what is base, and degrades what is costly."[2]

"Often he obliges us most who gives little, but equals kings in the richness of his heart, forgetting his own wants in beholding ours, and thinking that he is not so much conferring as receiving favors."[3]

"Let us give as we would receive, cheerfully, quickly, and unhesitatingly ; in a gift that sticks to the fingers there is no grace."[4]

"It is better to get the start of a request than to follow it."[5]

"He who gives when he is asked has waited too long."[6]

"Great favors are often spoilt by being given slowly and sadly, and as if they were refused."[7]

---

[1] *Seneca's De Beneficiis*, book i, chap. ii, sec. 3; [2] book i, chap. vi, sec. 2; [3] book i, chap. vii, sec. 1; [4] book ii, chap. i, secs. 1 and 2; [5] book ii, chap. i, sec. 3; [6] book ii, chap. ii, sec. 1; [7] book ii, chap. iii, sec. 1.

"Nothing is so painful as long suspense. What you add to the delay you take from the gratitude."[1]

"He who gives gladly gives quickly; he who delays, loses not only his time, but his chance of proving his friendship."[2]

"It is best that those who are helped should not know their benefactor, for the secrecy increases the gift."[3]

"A man who boasted everywhere of his kind actions was told, 'You have had your pay for them all.' 'When?' he asked. 'Whenever you have told about them.'"[4]

"He is best who gives readily, and asks nothing in return, but takes whatever is offered gladly, and feels himself obliged, because he has forgotten his own gift."[5]

"Covetousness permits no gratitude."[6]

"Give the kindness for its own sake; thinking only of the receiver's interests."[7]

[1] *Seneca's De Beneficiis*, book ii, chap. v, secs. 1 and 2 (the last part quoted from a comic poet); [2] book ii, chap. v, sec. 4; [3] book ii, chap. x, sec. 2; [4] book ii, chap. xi, sec. 2; [5] book ii, chap. xvii, sec. 7; [6] book ii, chap. xxvii, sec. 3; [7] book iv, chap. ix, sec. 1.

"The wise man will give not only to those who are good, but to those whom he can make so; he will choose out the worthiest with the utmost care, and never give without sufficient reason; for unwise gifts must be reckoned among foolish extravagances; his purse will open easily, but never leak."[1]

"He errs who thinks it easy to give alms; it is very difficult, if they are to be distributed with any purpose, and not merely thrown away by chance. To some I will give nothing, because, however much they might get, they would always be in want; while on others I would press, and even force, my gifts. Never do I take more pains in any investments than in these."[2]

"Prodigality is never noble, and especially not in charity."[3]

"Let no one suppose that I would check charity; let it go where it will, but not wander to and fro."[4]

---

[1] *Seneca's Dialogues,* book vii, chap. xxiii, sec. 5; [2] book vii, chap. xxiv, sec. 1. [3] *De Beneficiis,* book i, chap. ii, sec. 1; [4] book i, chap. xiv, sec. 2.

"As no impulse, though arising from good intentions, is good, unless properly directed, I forbid that charity should be squandered."[1]

"Giving to a base man is neither noble nor generous."[2]

"What is given imprudently is lost culpably, and more so for doing no good than for making no return."[3]

"The wise man considers to whom he gives, rather than what he gives."[4]

"He helps his friends, not through his own strength, but through theirs."[5]

"All agree that some gifts should be given publicly, and others secretly. Thus, prizes of valor, and honors, and whatever else gains value by being known, should be bestowed publicly; but what does not bring glory, but only keeps off weakness, poverty, and shame, should be given in silence, and known only to those who are relieved."[6]

[1] *Seneca's De Beneficiis*, book i, chap. xv, sec. 3; [2] book iv, chap. ix, sec. 3; [3] book iv, chap. x, sec. 3. [4] *Epistles*, xix, sec. 12; [5] *Ep.* cix, sec. 6. [6] *De Benef.*, book ii, chap. ix, secs. 1 and 2.

"I shall give nothing for which I would be ashamed to ask."[1]

"There is no kindness in giving, but only in denying, what would injure him who asks for it. Not his wish, but his welfare, is to be considered."[2]

"To let others beg us into ruining them is a cruel kindness, a smooth and flattering hatred, just as to save those who do not wish to be most noble."[3]

"Often the friends give exactly what the enemies wish."[4]

"Delight in acts of kindness is our nearest approach to the divine."[5]

"Thrasea used to say that we should take the side not only of our friends, but of the friendless."[6]

"Animals who lack reason should be treated nobly and magnanimously."[7]

---

[1] *Seneca's De Beneficiis*, book ii, chap. xv, sec. 2; [2] book ii, chap. xiv, sec. 1; [3] book ii, chap. xiv, sec. 4; [4] book ii, chap. xiv, sec. 5.

[5] *Dion Chrysostom's De Regno II* (Wakefield, pp. 9-10), vol. i, p. 25.

[6] *Pliny's Epistles*, xxix, book vi, sec. 1.

[7] *Marcus Aurelius' Meditations*, book vi, sec. 23.

PATRIOTISM.

"The true philosopher, unless prevented, will serve the state."[1]

"Of all ties, none is closer and dearer than that between our country and ourselves. Our parents, children, kinsmen and friends are dear to us, but they are all comprehended in our country, and for her what good man would hesitate to die?"[2]

"Those in charge of public business should look at the advantage of the citizens, and follow that, in all they do, forgetting themselves. Such a trust should be administered in the interest of those who give it, not that of him to whom it is given."[3]

"Nobly spoke our own Rutilius to those who tried to console him, when he was going into banishment, by saying that he would soon be called back, by the coming civil war: 'What evil have I done to you, that you should wish me a return worse than this de-

---

[1] *Zeno*, in *Seneca's Dialogues*, book viii, chap. iii, sec. 2.
[2] *Panætius*, in *Cicero's De Officiis*, book i, chap. xvii, sec. 12; [3] book i, chap. xxv, secs. 1 and 2.

parture? Better to have my country blush at my exile, than weep over my recall.'"[1]

"I fight, not for my own liberty, but for my country's; not to live free, but to live among freemen."[2]

"Not only he who brings forward candidates, defends the accused, and decides about peace and war, serves the state, but also he who instructs the young, forms their minds to virtue, and hinders their rushing into dissipation or avarice."[3]

"Does the prætor do more for the public than he who teaches what is justice, piety, patience, courage, scorn of death, and knowledge of the gods, and how great is the value of a good conscience?"[4]

"If fortune prevent the philosopher from being active in politics, he will not throw down his arms and run away into some hiding place; but he will look about carefully, and do his best to find some way to be useful to his country."[5]

[1] *Seneca's De Beneficiis*, book vi, chap. xxxvii, sec. 2. [2] *Cato*, in *Seneca's Epistles*, xxiv, sec. 7. [3] *Seneca's Dialogues*, book ix, chap. iii, sec. 3; [4] book ix, chap. iii, sec. 4; [5] book ix, chap. iv, sec. 2.

"No one loves his country because she is great, but because she is his own."[1]

"Let private interests yield to public, the mortal to the eternal."[2]

"What would I have death find me doing? Something benevolent, public - spirited, and noble."[3]

"No philosopher should refuse to take part in the government, for it is base to give way to the worthless, wicked to turn away from those who need our help, and foolish to prefer being ruled ill to ruling well."[4]

"Fear nothing, but that thy mind should turn to something unworthy of a thinker and a citizen."[5]

"'If thou wouldst have peace, busy thyself with but few things,' said Democritus. We should rather say, Busy thyself with all that needs to be done and that belongs to thee as a member of the community."[6]

[1] *Seneca's Epistles*, lxvi, sec. 26.

[2] *Pliny's Epistles*, xviii, book vii, sec. 5.

[3] *Epictetus' Discourses*, book iv, chap. x, sec. 12. [4] *Fragments*, cxxxi, in Didot.

[5] *Marcus Aurelius' Meditations*, book iii, sec. 7; [6] book iv, sec. 24.

"That harms not the citizen which does not harm the state."[1]

"He who values his own soul, which is both philanthropic and patriotic, cares for nothing except to keep himself reasonable and public-spirited."[2]

"That which is not good for the swarm is not good for the bee."[3]

"Whatever I can do ought to be directed to this end alone—usefulness to the community."[4]

"A reasoning being goes on his way well, when he directs his impulses only to actions of public benefit."[5]

. "Every act of thine which is without any immediate or ultimate reference to the welfare of the community tears thy life asunder."[6]

"Let thy efforts and exertions be turned toward acting for the public good."[7]

"Thou art a man set at thy post for the benefit of the state."[8]

---

[1] *Marcus Aurelius' Meditations*, book v, sec. 22; [2] book vi, sec. 14; [3] book vi, sec. 54; [4] book vii, sec. 5; [5] book viii, sec. 7; [6] book ix, sec. 23; [7] book ix, sec. 31; [8] book xi, sec. 13 (addressed to himself as emperor).

"Our object should be the good of the state and of the community."[1]

"Do nothing without a purpose, and let that always be some public end."[2]

PHILANTHROPY.

"Love is the god who gives safety to the city."[3]

"I will show you how to make a love-potion without either drugs or spells : If you would be loved, love."[4]

"We are created for the sake of mankind, to be useful to each other."[5]

"Nature endears man to man."[6]

"Nothing is more natural to man than kindness."[7]

"All men are plainly bound together."[8]

"Knowledge seems isolated and barren,

[1] *Marcus Aurelius' Meditations*, book xi, sec. 21; [2] book xii, sec. 20.

[3] *Zeno*, quoted in *Denis' Histoire des Theories Morales*, vol. i, p. 346.

[4] *Hecaton*, quoted in *Seneca's Epistles*, ix, sec. 6.

[5] *Cicero's De Officiis*, book i, chap. vii, sec. 5; [6] book i, chap. iv, sec. 4, and also *Epictetus' Discourses*, book iii, chap. xxiv, sec. 11. [7] *De Off.*, book i, chap. xiv, sec. 1; [8] book i, chap. xvi, sec. 5.

unless accompanied by love of all men and trust in our common brotherhood.'[1]

"Obey that law of nature which makes your interest the universal, and the universal one your own."[2]

"The same law of nature binds us all together."[3]

"They who say that we should love our fellow-citizens, but not foreigners, destroy the universal brotherhood of mankind, with which benevolence and justice would perish.[4]

"Care for other men and serve the common brotherhood.[5]

"It is because he is a man, that no other man should seem to me a stranger. All the universe is a city where gods and men dwell together; Nature bids us prefer the general interest to our own, and consider the welfare of those who will come after us. We are born for fellowship with other men, and

---

[1] *Cicero's De Officiis*, book i, chap. xliv, sec. 8. [2] *Antipater Tyrius*, quoted in *De Off.*, book iii, chap. vi, sec 1, and chap. xii, sec. 7. [3] *De Off*, book iii, chap. vi, sec. 3; [4] book iii, chap. vi, sec. 6. [5] *Antipater Tyrius*, quoted in *De Off.*, book iii, chap. xii, sec. 7.

forced by nature to wish to benefit as many people as possible, especially by teaching them wisdom."[1]

"Men are made for helping each other."[2]

"I shall take the world as my country."[3]

"Nature commands me to do good to all men, whether they be bond or free."[4]

"We will continue active until the end of life, and not cease to labor for the common good, but aid each individual, and succor even our enemies with our aged hands."[5]

"Think of that great republic whose boundary is the course of the sun, and whose citizens are all the men and gods."[6]

"The wise man looks upon himself as the citizen and soldier of the universe."[7]

"Let us have such noble souls as not to shut ourselves up within a single city, but take an interest in all the countries of the earth."[8]

---

[1] *Cato*, quoted in *Cicero's De Finibus*, book iii, chap. xix, secs. 63-4, and chap. xx, sec. 65.

[2] *Seneca's Dialogues*, book iii, chap. v, sec. 2; [3] book vii, chap. xx, sec. 5; [4] book vii, chap. xxiv, sec. 3; [5] book viii, chap. i, sec. 4; [6] book viii, chap. iv, sec. 1. [7] *Epistles*, cxx, sec. 12   [8] *Dial.*, book ix, chap. iv, sec. 4.

"Man is created to live in society and for the common good."[1]

"The Stoic rule of life is to be useful and helpful, and not look after ourselves alone, but after the individual and common interests of all mankind."[2]

"And this it is that binds society together."[3]

"How could we be safe, if we did not help each other and interchange kindnesses? Make us solitary and what should we be? A prey to other animals, and most easy victims. It is society that has given man dominion over them, and bade him rule the sea; she arms him against disease, supports him in old age, and consoles him in sorrow. Take away society, and you destroy that unity of the race which is the basis of life."[4]

"If you would live for yourself, live for others."[5]

"I enjoy learning, because I wish to teach;

[1] *Seneca's De Clementia*, book i, chap. iii, sec. 2; [2] book ii, chap. v, sec. 3. [3] *De Beneficiis*, book i, chap. iv, sec. 2; [4] book iv, chap. xviii, secs. 1, 2, 3 and 4. [5] *Epistles*, xlviii, sec. 2.

no knowledge, however rare and useful, would please me, if it could be made known to no one else ; if wisdom were given me to be kept shut up within myself, and never uttered, I should cast it away."[1]

"We, Stoics, when shut out from politics, have devoted ourselves to elevating our own lives, and giving laws to our race."[2]

"Guard religiously that social tie which binds man to man, and establishes the rights common to the human race."[3]

"Wisdom looks on every man as a friend, but folly will not even look on a friend as a man."[4]

"The wise man has a country worthy of him, the universe, out of which he cannot go."[5]

"Philanthropy forbids us to be proud or bitter with any one ; she makes all our deeds and words and feelings kind, and thinks no evil, even of a stranger."[6]

"Philosophy teaches love of man, preaches

[1] *Seneca's Epistles*, vi, sec. 4; [2] *Ep.* xiv, sec. 14; [3] *Ep.* xlviii, sec. 3; [4] *Ep.* xlviii, sec. 4; [5] *Ep.* lxviii, sec. 2; [6] *Ep* lxxxviii, sec. 30.

peace, and calls on the whole human race to live in harmony." [1]

"The weak grow strong in union, but the mighty perish by discord." [2]

"This is the rule of duty. Nature has bound us together as kindred, implanted in us mutual love, and made us kindly affectioned, so that it is more painful for us to injure than to be injured. She bids our helpful hands be ever ready. Let us have this verse ever on our lips and in our hearts:

'I'm human. So I think no other man a stranger.'

We are made to live together; humanity is an arch which falls unless each part sustains the rest." [3]

"Human life consists in kindness and harmony, and is bound together for mutual help, not by terror, but by love." [4]

"It belongs to a citizen of the universe to have no private interests, and to think

---

[1] *Seneca's Epistles*, xc, secs. 3 and 26; [2] *Ep.* xciv, sec. 46; [3] *Ep* xcv, secs. 52 and 53. (The quotation is from Terence: "Homo sum, humani nihil a me alienum puto."—Heautontimorumenos, act i, scene i, line 25.) [4] *Dialogues*, book iii, chap. v, sec. 3.

of nothing without reference to the general good."[1]

"If you have changed from a man, a mild and philanthropic being, into a wild beast, a treacherous and destructive creature, have you lost nothing? Must you lose money in order to suffer loss?"[2]

"There is a natural fellowship among men, and it ought in every way to be preserved."[3]

"Meditate upon your actions. Ask yourself, 'What have I done that is contrary to the interests of my friends and of my race?'"[4]

"Man's nature is to do good and assist others and comply with their wishes."[5]

"No one who is a lover of money, pleasure, or fame, is also a lover of mankind, but only he who is a lover of virtue."[6]

"Nothing is meaner than love of money, fame, or pleasure. Nothing is nobler than greatness of mind, gentleness and philanthropy."[7]

[1] *Epictetus' Discourses*, book ii, chap. x, sec. 4; [2] book ii, chap. x, sec. 14; [3] book ii, chap. xx, sec. 8; [4] book iv, chap. vi, sec. 35; [5] book iv, chap. i, sec. 122. [6] *Fragments*, xiii (Didot); [7] *Frag.*, li (Didot).

"As the sun does not wait for prayers and witcheries before rising, but shines forth immediately, welcome to every one, so should you not wait for applause and praise before doing good, but be a benefactor of your own accord, and so be loved like the sun."[1]

"A man, who was reproached for doing good to a shipwrecked pirate, answered: 'It was not the man I honored, but mankind.'"[2]

"We are made for co-operation, like the hands and feet."[3]

"Does any one hate me? I will be kind and friendly to every one."[4]

"Keep thyself from all thoughts which thou canst not confess openly, so that thy words may show thee wholly frank and loving, as a social being should be, caring not for sensual pleasure, and free from rivalry, envy, or suspicion. Such a man is a priest of the gods, and a champion in the noblest fight. He knows that every rational being is

---

[1] *Epictetus' Fragments*, lxxxviii (Didot); [2] *Frag.*, cix (Didot).
[3] *Marcus Aurelius' Meditations*, book ii, sec. 1; [4] book xi, sec. 13.

his kinsman, and that it is part of his own nature to care for all men." [1]

"Do not labor unwillingly, or without regard to the common good." [2]

"God gives man power never to let himself be separated from the great whole." [3]

"Do nothing but what is useful to men." [4]

"It is like a deserter to flee away from social laws." [5]

"The chief end of a rational creature is the social life." [6]

"Put all thy joy and satisfaction in passing from one philanthropic action to another, thinking of God." [7]

"Treat men fraternally, because they are endowed with reason." [8]

"My nature is thoughtful and patriotic; and my country, as I am an Antonine, is Rome, but as I am a man it is the Cosmos. Only what is useful to these countries is useful to me." [9]

[1] *Marcus Aurelius' Meditations*, book iii, sec. 4; [2] book iii, sec. 5; [3] book viii, sec. 34; [4] book iv, sec. 12; [5] book iv, sec. 29; [6] book v, sec. 16; [7] book vi, sec. 7; [8] book vi, sec. 23; [9] book vi, sec. 44.

"Love mankind." [1]

"Rational creatures exist for each other's good; for which reason our first duty is to be philanthropic, and our second is not to yield to bodily desire." [2]

"Peculiarly manly is benevolence to our fellow-men." [3]

"Say often to thyself, I am an active member of the society of beings who reason, for to think of thyself merely as helped on by it is neither to love men with all thy heart, nor to find thy pleasure simply in doing good." [4]

[1] *Marcus Aurelius' Meditations*, book vii, sec. 31; [2] book vii, sec. 55; [3] book viii, sec. 26; [4] book vii, sec. 13.

CHAPTER VI.

MAXIMS OF JUSTICE.

OF these I could collect comparatively few, though this chapter includes the subjects of Honesty, Fidelity, Respect for Others' Rights, Obeying and Enforcing the Laws, and Speaking the Truth.. Stoicism is commonly supposed to have been both more austere and less humane than it was in reality.

HONESTY.

"More beautiful than all temples is that cottage where dwell justice, self-control, prudence, piety, proper regard for all duties, and knowledge of all that is human or divine." [1]

"He is not honest who cares for any-thing in this virtue except itself." [2]

"To be honest simply for the sake of being so is too little; we should delight in sacrificing ourselves for this most lovely of virtues." [3]

"Often our duty is to be just and reputed infamous." [4]

"Give no judgment from any other tribunal, before you have yourself been judged at that of Justice." [5]

"If you would judge justly, esteem neither parties nor pleaders, but the case itself." [6]

"Better to be blamed for a just judgment by him who is condemned, than to be degraded for an unjust one by Nature herself." [7]

"As the touchstone tries gold, but is not itself tried by it, so is he who has the power of judging justly." [8]

[1] *Seneca's Dialogues*, book xii, chap. ix, sec. 3.   [2] *Epistles*, xciv, sec. 11; [3] *Ep.* cxiii, sec. 31; [4] *Ep.* cxiii, sec. 32.

[5] *Epictetus' Fragments*, lx (Didot); [6] *Frag.*, lxi (Didot); [7] *Frag.*, lxiii (Didot); [8] *Frag.*, lxiv (Didot).

"Every place is safe for him who dwells with justice."[1]

"Not even the choicest friendship is free from passions which may overshadow and disturb thy sense of justice."[2]

"Thou mayst pass thy life in constant happiness, if thou wilt follow these two rules: not to let thyself be hindered by others, and not to desire anything except to seek and do what is honest."[3]

"Not yet dost thou see that prudence is all contained in justice."[4]

"All the other virtues spring from justice; for this cannot be preserved, if we think too much of other things, or let ourselves be deceived easily, or are hasty in forming and changing our opinions."[5]

FIDELITY.

"The holiest possession of the human soul is that fidelity which is corrupted by no reward, and forced to deceive by no necessity."[6]

---

[1] *Epictetus' Fragments*, cii (Didot); [2] *Frag.*, cxxxix (Didot).
[3] *Marcus Aurelius' Meditations*, book v, sec. 34; [4] book iv, sec. 37; [5] book xi, sec. 10.
[6] *Seneca's Epistles*, lxxxviii, sec. 29.

"He is wicked who does not practise that chastity which he requires from his wife."[1]

"Prosperity invites our fidelity; adversity demands it."[2]

"The faith which expects rewards is to be conquered by them."[3]

"Act well to present friends; speak well of absent ones."[4]

"My word is as my country to me, and even dearer, if anything can be."[5]

RESPECT FOR OTHERS' RIGHTS.

"Whether the slave have become so by conquest or by purchase, the master's title is bad."[6]

"Let thy slaves laugh, or talk, or be silent, in thy presence, as in that of the father of the family."[7]

---

[1] *Seneca's Epistles*, xciv, sec. 26.   [2] Speech of Strophius, in the *Agamemnon*, supposed to be by Seneca, line 13.   [3] Speech of Aegisthus, in the *Agamemnon*, supposed to be by Seneca, line 287.

[4] *Epictetus' Fragments*, clv, in Didot.

[5] *Pliny's Epistles*, xviii, book i, sec. 4.

[6] *Zeno*, quoted in *Denis' Histoire des Theories Morales*, vol. 1, p. 346.

[7] *Seneca's Dialogues*, book v, chap. xxxv, sec. 2.

"I will lessen no one's liberty."[1]

"He who denies that a slave can do a kindness to his master ignores the law of nature. It matters not what station a man has, but what disposition. Virtue is free and open to all; she admits and invites everybody, slaves or freemen, exiles or kings; she has no preference for family or property, but is satisfied with the mere man."[2]

"One universe is our common parent. Do not despise any one because he is surrounded by vulgar names, or unfavored by fortune."[3]

"The first law of friendship is equality."[4]

"Philosophy neither accepts nor rejects any one, but shines for all."[5]

"To live familiarly with your slaves, shows, not only that you are educated, but that you are wise; they are slaves, but they are also men, and friends, and our fellow-servants."[6]

"Remember that he whom thou callest

---

[1] *Seneca's Dialogues*, book vii, chap. xx, sec. 5. [2] *De Beneficiis*, book iii, chap. xviii, sec. 2; [3] book iii, chap. xxviii, secs. 2 and 3; [4] book ii, chap. xv, sec. 1. [5] *Epistles*, xliv, sec. 2; [6] *Ep.* xlvii, sec. 1.

thy slave is born of the same race as thy-self, lives the same life, and dies the same death. Wilt thou despise a man for circum-stances which may become thine own?"[1]

"Live with thy inferiors as thou wouldst have thy superiors live with thee."[2]

"Have thy slaves honor, rather than fear, thee. Punish them only with words."[3]

"Virtue may be born in any place."[4]

"Justice considers only the good of oth-ers, and desires nothing but to be of use."[5]

"Let us not charge any one with base-ness of birth. Let us have free laborers, and think their labors useful and noble."[6]

"Do you consider him a small offender who makes a man more corrupt?"[7]

. Pliny, on being asked if he followed the custom of serving some guests at dinner with much better food and wine than the rest, said : "I set the same before everybody, for

[1] Seneca's Epistles, xlvii, sec. 10; [2] Ep. xlvii, sec. 11; [3] Ep. xlvii, secs. 18 and 19; [4] Ep. lxvi, sec. 3; [5] Ep. cxiii, sec. 31.

[6] Dion Chrysostom, quoted in Champigny's Les Antonins, vol. 1, p. 428.

[7] Dion Chrysostom's De Servis, vol. i, p. 159.

I regard all whom I invite to my table, even my servants, as equals." [1]

"In using the power of a father, remember not only that your son is a boy, as you have been, but that you are a man, and the father of one." [2]

"Will you not remember that your servants are by nature your brothers, the children of God? In saying that you have bought them, you look down on the earth, and into the pit, on the wretched laws of men long since dead, but you see not the laws of the gods." [3]

"What you would not suffer yourself take care not to impose on others; and as you would escape slavery, do not treat others like slaves." [4]

"From Diognetus I learned to endure freedom of speech." [5]

"I have formed the ideal of a state in

---

[1] *Pliny's Epistles*, vi, book ii, sec. 3; [2] *Ep.* xii, book ix, sec. 2.

[3] *Epictetus' Discourses*, book i, chap. xiii, secs. 4 and 5.
[4] *Fragments*, xlii, in Didot.

[5] *Marcus Aurelius' Meditations*, book i, sec. 6.

which there is the same law for all, and equal
rights and equal liberty of speech are established, an empire where nothing is honored
so much as the freedom of the citizens." [1]

OBEYING AND ENFORCING THE LAWS.

" To pardon everybody is as cruel as to
pardon nobody." [2]

" The wise man will not pardon any crime
which ought to be punished, but he will accomplish in a nobler way all that is sought
in pardoning : he will spare, watch over and
reform some because of their youth, and others on account of their ignorance. His clem-
ency will not fall short of justice, but only
fulfill it perfectly." [3]

" It is absurd to lose our own innocence
rather than to do harm to other people." [4]

" Peace with all mankind, but war with
vice." [5]

" He who spares the bad wrongs the good." [6]

---

[1] *Marcus Aurelius' Meditations*, book i, sec. 14.

[2] *Seneca's De Clementia*, book i, chap. ii, sec. 2 ; [3] book ii,
chap, vii, secs. 1, 2 and 3. [4] *De Moribus*, sec. 17 ; [5] sec. 34.
[6] sec. 114.

"He who will not forbid sin commands it."[1]

"The law aims to do men good, but this it cannot accomplish unless they are willing; only to the obedient is its virtue shown."[2]

"It is beautiful to yield to a law, to a ruler, or to a wiser man."[3]

SPEAKING THE TRUTH.

"The possessor of all things else may need a friend to tell him the truth, and free him from the conspiracy of falsehood."[4]

"It is base to say, and baser still to write, what we do not feel."[5]

"Truth hates delay."[6]

"If you seek truth, you will not wish to conquer by all sorts of means; and if you find truth, you will never be conquered."[7]

"Truth conquers by itself, opinion by appealing to externals."[8]

---

[1] Speech of Agamemnon in the *Tragades*, supposed to be by Seneca, line 291.

[2] *Epictetus' Fragments*, cxxii (Didot); [3] *Frag.*, cxxv (Didot).

[4] *Seneca's De Beneficiis*, book vi, chap. xxx, sec. 3. [5] *Epistles*, xxiv, sec. 19. [6] Speech of Œdipus in the *Œdipus*, supposed to be by Seneca, line 871.

[7] *Epictetus' Fragments*, xxxix (Didot); [8] *Frag.*, xl (Didot).

"Let nothing be more precious to thee than truth."[1]

"Flatterers destroy the souls of men by blinding their eyes."[2]

"Be on thy guard equally against being angry at others and against flattering them, for to do either is to neglect the common welfare and inflict injury."[3]

"The safety of life demands that I do what is just with my whole soul, and say what is true."[4]

"To act a part, or say or do anything insincere or untrue, pollutes the soul."[5]

"Think nothing profitable which will ever force thee to break thy word, to lose thy self-respect, to hate, suspect, curse or deceive any one, or to desire anything that need be covered with walls or veils."[6]

"There is no veil over a star."[7]

[1] *Epictetus' Fragments*, cxxxix (Didot); [2] *Frag.*, ciii (Didot).
[3] *Marcus Aurelius' Meditations*, book xi, sec. 18; [4] book xii, sec. 29; [5] book ii, sec. 16; [6] book iii, sec. 7; [7] book xi, sec. 27.

CHAPTER VII.

PHILOSOPHY.

TO omit this subject would be like leaving out the part of Hamlet, but as few of my readers might care for a lengthy disquisition, I will do little more than give my general conclusions, with the necessary quotations and references.

Some space must, first of all, be given to a question about which there is still a controversy, namely: whether the Stoics recognized intuitions and innate ideas, or, in other words, the conscience, as the supreme revelation of duty, or whether they held a position intermediate between that of Plato and Epicurus. Philosophers holding this latter position, and also a theology so strongly transcendental as that of the Stoics, might be expected to furnish many passages which look like utterances of the intuitive morality, especially when we allow for what may be added inadvertently by the translators. Thus Miss Cobbe, on the 120th page of her *Intuitive Morals*, brings forward some lines from Rowe's *Lucan* which owe all their special significance to two words, "inborn precepts," that have no equivalent in the original Latin, all whose meaning is preserved by that part of the version which has been given on page 69 of this book.

That the Stoics, while holding some theological views similar to Miss Cobbe's, and still more so to those of Ralph Waldo Emerson, were anything but transcendental in their ethics and metaphysics, I infer from the following facts:

First, our best authority about the early Stoics, Cicero, declares repeatedly that they followed that illustrious early opponent of innate ideas, Aristotle, so closely as to be charged with stealing all his teachings, and altering merely the terms, as thieves do the marks on stolen goods.[1]

And, second, Plutarch always treats the Stoics as opponents to his master, Plato, and declares that they taught, as Locke did afterward, "that the mind of man is a sheet of writing-paper, on which the first writing is done by the senses," and also "that ideas are nothing else but the conceptions of our own minds."[2]

Then, third, we find in Seneca and Epictetus many passages which are especially significant when we consider how unwillingly the extreme idealists, like Plato and Parker, have been to admit that the conscience could be educated or virtue taught.[3]

Some of the most important will be found on pages 142 and 143. Others are these:

[1] *De Finibus*, book v, chap. xxv, sec. 74; and book iv, chap. xxvi, sec. 72.

[2] *Plutarch's Morals*, Goodwin's Ed., vol. iii, pp. 123, 166: The Sentiments of Nature, book i, chap. x.

[3] *The Dialogues of Plato*, translated by B. Jowett, vol. i, pp. 275-6. *The Life of Theodore Parker*, by John Weiss, vol. i, p. 108.

"No impulse is good, unless properly controlled, however good the intention which prompts it."[1]

"We cannot expect to comprehend anything perfectly, for truth is hard to find, but we must go where the appearance of truth leads, guided by what is reasonable, rather than by what is certain."[2]

"It is hard to find virtue, and there is need of governors and guides."[3]

"No one can do his duties properly unless he has learnt that general principle by which he can find them out in all particulars."[4]

"No one has strength enough of his own to rise out of folly; one must give another the hand."[5]

"The soul should be taught to follow some model, like boys who learn to write."[6]

"He is good whose reason is developed, and corrected, and conformed to the will of Nature."[7]

---

[1] *Seneca's De Beneficiis*, book i, chap. xv, sec. 3; [2] book iv, chap. xxxiii, sec. 2. [3] *Naturalium Quæstionum*, book iii, chap. xxx, sec. 8. [4] *Epistles*, xcv, sec. 12; [5] *Ep.* lii, sec. 2; [6] *Ep.* xciv, sec. 51; [7] *Ep.* lxxvi, sec. 15.

"Liberal studies prepare the mind for accepting virtue."[1]

"The character does not become perfect without that abiding knowledge of good and evil which only philosophy can give."[2]

"It is the gift of the immortal gods that we live, and of philosophy that we live well; and it is they who give her, not the knowledge of her to any one, but the power of learning to all."[3]

"Her sole business is to find out the truth about all that is human or divine, and she it is who teaches us to worship the gods, and love mankind."[4]

"Nature does not give virtue, but it is an art to become good."[5]

"Virtue does not come. until the character is formed, and taught, and developed by continual exercise."[6]

"It is through the parts that we must reach the whole."[7]

---

[1] *Seneca's Epistles*, lxxxviii, sec. 20; [2] *Ep.* lxxxviii, sec. 28; [3] *Ep.* xc, sec. 1; [4] *Ep.* xc, sec. 3; [5] *Ep.* xc, sec. 44; [6] *Ep.* xc, sec. 46; [7] *Ep.* cviii, sec. 2.

"He gives no promise of remaining virtuous who is so by accident."[1]

"How has the first knowledge of goodness and virtue come to us? Nature could not teach us this. She gave us the germs of knowledge, but not the knowledge itself. Our philosophy holds that these ideas come by observation and comparison of our daily deeds, and that goodness and virtue are known by analogy."[2]

"No one is good by accident; virtue must be learned."[3]

"What, then, is the cause of my sinning? Ignorance."[4]

"When we would judge of weights, or whether anything is straight or crooked, we do not decide at random. And whenever it is important for us to know the truth, nobody would decide without deliberation. But here, where there is the first and only cause of our acting virtuously or sinfully, failing or suc-

[1] *Seneca's Epistles,* xcv, sec. 39; [2] *Ep.* cxx, secs. 3 and 4; [3] *Ep.* cxxiu, sec. 16.

[4] *Epictetus' Discourses,* book i, chap. xxvi, sec. 7.

ceeding, and being happy or miserable, then alone do we act without deliberation and hastily. Nowhere anything like a rule or a balance, but something seems right to me, and I do it at once. What do we call those who follow every appearance? Madmen."[1]

"Let us come to some stronger ground than mere belief. Philosophy begins in our being aware of the differences of men among themselves, inquiring into the cause of these differences, disapproving and distrusting mere beliefs, examining them to see how far they are correct, and finally finding out some test which shall serve us, as the balance does, in telling what is light or heavy, or the rule, in showing what is crooked or straight. This is the beginning of philosophy. It is impossible that beliefs which are held differently by different people, and in which we differ from the Syrians and Egyptians, can be correct. And even in weights and measures we are not satisfied with the mere appearance, but for everything we have some test. Is it possible

[1] *Epictetus' Discourses*, book i, chap. xxviii, secs. 28–33.

that what is of the greatest importance to
mankind should have no test and be past our
finding out ?   There is a test, then ; and why
not seek for it and find it, and then use it
unceasingly, so as never to stir a finger without it ?   Thus can those who use no test but
their own belief be cured of. their madness.
It is the business of philosophy to exam-
ine and fix these tests ; and to make use
of those which are known is the part of a
good and wise man." [1]

"What makes a man free and master of
himself?   The science of living." [2]

"Burn the midnight oil to gain principles
which will set you free." [3]

And, fourth, this evidence will be found
still stronger after inquiring what "following
nature" really meant to the Stoics.   These
philosophers used the word in two senses :
first, of the visible universe of phenomena ;
and second, of its Invisible Ruler, that highest object of worship and obedience, called

----

[1] *Epictetus' Discourses*, book ii, chap. xi, secs. 12–25; [2] book
iv, chap. i, secs. 62 and 63; [3] book iv, chap. i, sec. 176.

by Emerson the Over-Soul, and by Herbert Spencer the Unknowable Reality. These two significations were afterward distinguished as the *natura naturata* and the *Natura Naturans.* The Stoics believed in the profoundest obedience to the *Natura Naturans,* but when they would find out what this supreme power commanded, they looked not at their own intuitions, but at the revelations in the *natura naturata,* and especially at the laws of human nature, and the conditions of social welfare and universal happiness. That this is the fact is proved by the following quotations, to which many similar ones might be added:

"Neither any of the virtues is eligible, nor any of the vices to be avoided, for itself, but all these things are to be referred to the promised scope."[1]

"They hold the essence of good to be the reasonable election of things according to nature," or, "as they say, a reasonable election of things having a fitness for the causing fe-

[1] *Chrysippus,* quoted in *Plutarch's Morals,* Goodwin's Ed., vol. iv, p. 443.

licity.   This so highly venerated utility, which, preserving as some great and excellent thing for the wise, they permit not so much as the name of it to the vicious—this is the work of their amity; in this do the virtues of the wise man terminate by their common utilities." [1]

"The Stoics say that men are created for the sake of mankind, to be useful to each other; thus we are commanded to follow nature in being mutually and universally useful." [2]

"True philosophers have not neglected the advantage and interests of mankind." [3]

"Nothing does more to deprave human nature than the belief that anything is virtuous which is not useful, or useful which is not virtuous." [4]

"Panætius taught that virtue ought to be cultivated, because it is the cause of utility; that it is never at variance with real, but

[1] *Plutarch's Morals*, Goodwin's Ed., vol. iv, pp. 392, 399. Common Conceptions, chaps. xxii and xxvii.
[2] *Cicero's De Officiis*, book i, chap. vii, sec. 5; [3] book i, chap. xliv, sec. 1; [4] book ii, chap. ii, sec. 3.

only with imaginary, utility; that nothing is useful which is not also right, or right which is not also useful; and that no worse disease has ever invaded human life than the theory which disjoined these two ideas." [1]

"Duty is always performed when the advantage of mankind is sought." [2]

"Nothing is so much in accordance with nature as utility." [3]

"He is a good man who benefits as many people as possible, and harms nobody." [4]

"The standard of utility is the same as that of morality." [5]

"Those who separate utility and morality overthrow the fundamental principles of nature." [6]

"Whatever is really useful is virtuous, though it does not at first seem so." [7]

"In all our reasonings we should keep in view the general good." [8]

[1] *Cicero's De Officiis*, book iii, chap. iii, sec. 5, and chap. vii, sec. 6; [2] book iii, chap. vi, sec. 15; [3] book iii, chap. viii, sec. 2; [4] book iii, chap. xv, sec. 13; [5] book iii, chap. xviii, sec. 10; [6] book iii, chap. xxviii, secs. 1 and 2; [7] book iii, chap. xxviii, sec. 9, and chap. xxx, sec. 10.

[8] *Seneca's De Beneficiis*, book vii, chap. xvi, sec. 2.

"I owe more to humanity than to an individual."[1]

"In order to distinguish good from bad, you should consider, not whence it comes, but whither it tends. Whatever makes life happy is good by its own right, and cannot become evil."[2]

"Public and private utility are inseparable."[3]

"In being useful the soul moves according to nature."[4]

"Whatever is good is always profitable; if it does not profit, it is not good; if it does, it is so already."[5]

"To live happily is the same thing as to live according to nature."[6]

"No action of a depraved character, and destitute of utility, can prove unaccompanied by punishment."[7]

---

[1] *Seneca's De Beneficiis*, book vii, chap. xix, sec. 9. [2] *Epistles*, xliv, sec. 6; [3] *Ep.* lxvi, sec. 10; [4] *Ep.* cix, sec. 12; [5] *Ep.* cxvii, sec. 27. [6] *Dialogues*, book vii, chap. viii, sec. 2.

[7] *Dion Chrysostom's Orations, De Servitute et Libertate*, vol. i, p. 256.

"Consider the antecedents and the consequences of every action before you undertake it." [1]

"Every creature is created for disliking and fleeing from what is hurtful and the causes thereof, and again for seeking and admiring what seems beneficial and its causes." [2]

"When any one identifies his own interests with those of piety, virtue, country, parents, and friends, all these are secured; but whenever he places his interest in anything else than these, then all these perish, borne down by the weight of self-interest. For, wherever I and mine are placed, thither must every living creature gravitate." [3]

"God made all men to be happy and to be calm." [4]

"To be happy is a good object and one in your own power." [5]

"This, above all, is the business of nature, to bind the active powers together, and apply

[1] *Epictetus' Enchiridion*, chap. xxix, sec. 1; [2] chap. xxxi, sec. 3. [3] *Discourses*, book ii, chap. xxii, secs. 18 and 19; [4] book iii, chap. xxiv, sec. 2. [5] *Fragments*, xix (Didot).

them to what appears suitable and useful." [1]

"The soul dishonors herself whenever she does even the smallest act without a purpose." [2]

"Choose the better part; but that which is useful is the better part." [3]

"Do nothing which is not according to the principle that completes the art of life." [4]

"Repentance is a kind of self-reproof for having neglected something useful." [5]

"Let there be effort and exertion resulting in acting for the common good, for this, too, is according to thy nature." [6]

"If I remember that I am a part of the universe, I shall do nothing unsocial, but shall turn all my efforts to the common interest." [7]

"Do nothing inconsiderately or without a purpose." [8]

"And everything which is useful to the universe is always good and in season." [9]

---

[1] *Epictetus' Fragments*, lxix (Didot).

[2] *Marcus Aurelius' Meditations*, book ii, sec. 16; [3] book iii, sec. 6; [4] book iv, sec. 2; [5] book viii, sec. 10; [6] book ix, sec. 31; [7] book x, sec. 6; [8] book xii, sec. 20; [9] book xii, sec. 23.

These statements, which closely resemble some by John Stuart Mill, form, in connection with the quotations presented but just before, a strong array of evidence that the Stoics did not conceive of the moral sentiment, or idea of duty, as an atom or ultimate element, independent and incapable of analysis, but tried to analyze it into simpler elements. Such are my reasons for believing that these philosophers were not idealists or intuitionists, but held a place, as do the modern Utilitarians, in what the *Westminster Review* calls the derivative school of moralists.

And, lest the resemblance of Stoicism to Utilitarianism should seem doubtful, on account of the notorious hostility between the Stoics and the Epicureans, we must remember that the latter may fairly be called self-regarding, if not selfish. Their system had little encouragement for disinterestedness, or any other higher notion than desire for one's own independent happiness, while, practically, at least, it gave all the forms of pleasure, even the grossest, too much value. The Stoics, on the other hand, are proved by all their history and literature to have been in the highest degree disinterested, philanthropic, and devoted to the highest interests of all humanity. Seneca and Epictetus make clear distinctions between those forms of pleasure which are bodily, fleeting, uncertain, excessive, and therefore to be shunned, and those mental ones which are durable, certain, moderate, and should be cultivated; and that both these differences of Stoicism from Epicureanism brought it all the nearer to modern Utilitarianism, every reader of the ethical writings of J. S. Mill and Alexander Bain will easily see.

If we must hesitate about calling the Stoics utilitarians, it is not so much on account of anything they said, as on account of some things which they did not succeed in saying as clearly as they wished. For instance, they seem to have admitted that "the test for conduct should also be the exclusive motive to it," and thus to have fallen into the "error often, but falsely, charged against the whole class of utilitarian moralists."[1]

[1] Mill, Articles on Comte, p. 125.

This ignorance of the difference between taking utility only as a test, and making it not only a test, but also a motive, forced them sometimes to deny so sweepingly that it is the best motive as to disparage its value as a test, and at other times to use it as a test so incautiously as almost to sanction it as a motive.

They stated, in turn, most of the fundamental principles of the higher form of Utilitarianism, but they failed to combine these principles into that consistent system which may be thus built up. These apparent contradictions of the Stoics, together with the fondness of Marcus Aurelius for quoting Plato, and their general belief that it was irreverent to investigate closely the reasons why men should obey the Divine Will—a view in which they resembled Bishop Cumberland and Dr. Hopkins much more closely than more recent utilitarians—have made the discovery of their exact position in regard to the moral standard very difficult.

Another of their ethical theories, and the most characteristic of all, can be stated much

more briefly, though it has been much mis-
understood. They held that virtue was the
sole and sufficient cause of happiness, and
therefore the only strictly proper object of
desire, while the only thing always to be
shunned for its own sake was vice. Knowledge, indeed, was the essential condition of
goodness, and its acquisition the first of
the cardinal virtues. But forms of knowledge
which appeared lacking in ethical value were
disparaged by the Stoics, who attached little
importance to mechanical inventions or scientific investigations, and praised the primeval
Golden Age when they fancied that all men
did right unceasingly." [1]

Everything but knowledge and virtue—for
instance, health, riches, pleasure, political freedom, and life itself, like each of their opposites—occupied an intermediate position, being
strictly good only when it was a help to living virtuously, and bad whenever it became a
hindrance. Their scorn of these intermediate
things did not go so far as to lead them to
prefer poverty to riches, sickness to health,

---

[1] *Seneca's Epistles,* xc, *passim.*

despotism to liberty, or death to life, except when duty required such a choice, as in the case of what they thought a justifiable suicide. They made, indeed, the verbal error of calling all these things indifferent, but they admitted that, when no moral interest was at stake, there might properly be a preference of pleasure, health, wealth, liberty and life over their opposites, and to these advantages they gave terms equivalent to our word "preferable."

Passages have already been given, in chapter iv, which show that these philosophers were not ascetics. Chrysippus said: "They are mad who make no account of riches, health, freedom from pain, and integrity of the body, nor take any care to attain them."[1] Epictetus also taught that we should be like passengers who, in mid-ocean, go ashore and pick up what they like, but take care not to be left behind by the ship; or like guests at a banquet, who take a moderate share of what is set before them, but keep

---

[1] *Plutarch's Morals*, Goodwin's Ed., vol. iv, p. 457.

nothing standing by for private benefit, and desire nothing before it comes round." [1]

They recognized the fact that our happiness consists, first, in keeping calm and contented, despite all changes of fortune, improving our circumstances when we can, but submitting cheerfully to the inevitable; second, in restraining all desire to possess what we cannot get, or to have events take place otherwise than they do; third, in suppressing every passion that would lead to vice, and also every emotion which would cause pain to ourselves without giving others pleasure; fourth, so far as is consistent with such suppression and restraint, in cultivating our family affections, and friendly, social and patriotic feelings; and, fifth, in exerting our mental powers to the utmost degree compatible with these other conditions of felicity.

That the Stoics were not so unfeeling as they are often supposed to have been has frequently been shown in the above account of their history and teachings. Epictetus, indeed, says expressly: "I am not to be in

[1] *Enchiridion*, chaps. vii and xv.

apathy as a statue is, but as one who preserves not only his natural, but his acquired, relations, like a worshiper, a son, a brother, a father, a citizen."[1]

Of the glory and felicity of him who should fulfill these conditions of happiness they said far too much; but it must be remembered · that this perfectly wise man of theirs was simply an unattainable idol.

"Now, Chrysippus neither professes himself, nor any one of his disciples and teachers, to be virtuous."[2]

"We all have sinned; nor do we even give it up, but we go on offending until the end of life."[3]

"But show me a Stoic, if you have one. Who, then, is a Stoic? Show him to me, for, by the gods, I long to see a Stoic. Do not grudge an old man a sight which he has never yet seen."[4]

---

[1] *Discourses*, book iii, chap. ii, sec. 4.

[2] *Plutarch's Morals*, Goodwin's Ed., vol. iv, p. 459. *Contradictions of the Stoics*, chap. xxxi.

[3] *Seneca's De Clementia*, book i, chap. vi, sec. 3.

[4] *Epictetus' Discourses*, book ii, chap. xix, secs. 22, 24, 25.

"If anything could attach us to life, it would be to be able to live with people whose principles are like our own. But so sad is my disagreement with those around me, that I say, 'Come quick, O Death, lest I too forget myself.'"[1]

That the Stoics, like their contemporaries, believed in the four cardinal, or hinge, virtues of Wisdom, Temperance, Fortitude, and Justice, the latter including Benevolence; and that they also made a subdivision of duties, of their own, into what they called perfect and imperfect, and we may call absolute and relative, unconditional and conditional, or constant and occasional—need not be stated at length.

Such were their most important theories in ethics, which was, with all ancient philosophers, one of the three principal branches of philosophy, the other two being logic and physics. This latter was made by the Stoics to include theology and psychology, both of which were then usually made parts of logic.

---

[1] *Marcus Aurelius' Meditations*, book ix, sec. 3.

The early Stoics, while comparing philosophy
to an animal whose bones were logic, disa-
greed as to whether they should make ethics
the flesh and physics the soul, or vice versa.
Similar was the difference of opinion as to
which of these two rival studies, physics and
ethics, should be likened to the yolk, and
which to the white, in the egg of which ethics
was the shell. But gradually there came into
favor views according to which physics was the
trees in the orchard, ethics the fruit, and logic
the fence. But Epictetus is the only Stoic wri-
ter extant who valued the fence ; and neither
he nor Marcus Aurelius cared for the trees.

In what they called physics their chief
peculiarity was the belief that all that really
existed was substantial, and in some sense
even material. There was one universe, ruled
and pervaded by a Divine Soul, the Supreme
Reason, Immortal Nature, Destiny, and Providence. This Soul of the World also had its
substance, which the Stoics sometimes likened
to that of fire, not visible flame, but such invisible forms as the all-encompassing ether,
and the all-animating vital heat. Another

image, if nothing more, was that of the warm wind, or Spirit, the corresponding Latin title having the same root as our verb "respire," and the same relationship being found also in Hebrew and Greek. Peculiarly appropriate seemed the comparison to fire to philosophers who thought this the highest and noblest of all the elements, and the one from which the others had come forth, and into which all things would periodically return again. "Cleanthes is said to have followed Zeno in sometimes calling the universe itself God, at other times giving this name to the soul and spirit of all nature, and again in declaring that the highest, outermost and all surrounding heat, which is called the ether, is most certainly the Deity." [1]

"The Stoics thus define the essence of a God: It is a spirit, intellectual and fiery, which acknowledges no shape, but is continually changed into what it pleases, and assimilates itself to all things." [2]

---

[1] *Cicero's De Natura Decorum*, book i, chap. xiv, sec. 37.

[2] *Plutarch's Morals*, Goodwin's Ed., vol. iii, p. 115: Sentiments of Nature, book i, chap. vi.

"The Stoics affirm that God is a mechanic fire, which every way spreads itself to produce the world." [1]

"The elements may be destroyed by the operation of fire." [2]

"God himself they call a being who, after certain periods of time, absorbs all substance in himself, and then reproduces it from himself." [3]

A distinction, however, between God and matter is made in passages already quoted from Seneca, [4] who, like Epictetus and Marcus Aurelius, attached little importance to these materialistic conceptions, and dwelt rather on the wisdom and love of the Unseen and Incomprehensible God.

From this Being, as all the Stoics agreed, all things else have issued forth, including those lesser deities whose existence was accepted from the popular polytheism. And of this Supreme Spirit every human soul par-

---

[1] *Plutarch's Morals*, Goodwin's Ed., vol. iii, p. 122: Sentiments of Nature, book i, chap. vii.

[2] *Diogenes Laertius' Lives of the Philosophers*, p. 308;
[3] *Lives of the Philosophers*, p. 309.

[4] See page 66.

takes, and is thus distinct from the body, though nearly, if not wholly, identical with its vital heat; so that "the Stoics say it is a hot breath."[1]

They also believed, though not always confidently, in the survival of the soul after death until the final conflagration, when the Divine Nature would take all things back into itself again.

"The learned and vigorous endure until the general fire."[2]

"When the time shall come for the earth which is to be renewed to extinguish itself, then will all things perish by their own forces: star will rush against star, all matter will be in flames, and those luminaries which are now shining in their appointed places will blaze together in the same fire. And we, also, blessed souls who have attained immortality, shall, when it seems good to God to re-create

[1] *Plutarch's Morals*, Goodwin's Ed., vol. iii, p. 162: Sentiments of Nature, book iv, chap. iii.

[2] *Plutarch's Morals*, Goodwin's Ed., vol. iii, p. 164: Sentiments of Nature, book iv, chap. vii.

the world, return into our original elements, a small addition to so great a ruin." [1]

" The souls which are carried up into the air, after remaining there a while, are changed, dissolved, consumed, and absorbed into the Creative Reason." [2]

"Either there is a dissolution of the atoms, or there is a change of our body into earth and of our spirit into air, so that we pass into the Soul of the Universe, which latter is either consumed periodically or renewed in incessant changes." [3]

How far they were evolutionists, appears from this passage, and others on pages 60 and 64, as well as from their belief, that history kept repeating itself so literally that whatever took place in any one of the great periods which ended in conflagrations reappeared in every other, and that the same events kept recurring in generation after generation, so that he who had seen one had seen all.

" He who has seen the present has seen

[1] *Seneca's Dialogues*, book vi, chap. xxvi, secs. 6 and 7.
[2] *Marcus Aurelius' Meditations*, book iv, sec. 21; [3] book x, sec. 7.

everything which has ever been, or which will ever be, during all eternity; for all things are alike in nature and in form." [1]

Moral evil they thought a necessary result of the ignorance through which alone wisdom can be reached, and only a temporary one, to be finally removed by that Infinite Reason which always gives to every creature what is needed for its real and ultimate good. [2]

They taught that all events are guided by the Supreme Will, in a regular order, according to which all human actions are the necessary results of motives and desires, contrary to the modern theory of a self-determining will, choosing independent of motives—an opinion expressly combated by Chrysippus, who condemns the view that "this adventitious power of the soul, seizing on its inclinations, determines its actions"—as offering violence to Nature by devising an effect without a cause. [3]

[1] *Marcus Aurelius' Meditations,* book vi, sec. 37.

[2] See Hymn of Cleanthes, and similar passages, pp. 63–70.

[3] *Plutarch's Morals,* Goodwin's Ed., vol. iv, p. 452: Common Conceptions, chap. xxiii.

The Stoics greatly prized their own doctrine of Free Will, but this consisted, first, in asserting that each man's will was naturally independent of all things outside of himself; and, second, in directing that it should be kept so by the restriction of the desires to objects within their reach. This precept they thought the chief secret of happiness.

What they termed logic included disbelief in the real existence of ideas already mentioned. This led many of these admirers of virtue to the ridiculous fancy that, since it has a real existence, and actually exerts force, it is not merely ideal, but, in some sense, material; and, since it is not lifeless, it must be a living substance, or, in other words, an animal. Seneca, however, saw that virtue is simply a state of the soul, and utterly repudiated this error,[1] which, indeed, is not found in Epictetus or Marcus Aurelius.

Accordingly, the main principles may, with due allowance for the peculiar opinions of individuals, be summed up thus:

I. All that exists has material substance,

[1] *Epistles*, cxiii, secs. 2 and 7.

as is the case with the human mind, which receives its first impressions from the sensations, and therefrom produces all ideas.

II. Every human soul is a portion of that Divine Power, which is the soul of the world, unseen and incomprehensible, but yet resembling in substance heat, producing all things and creatures out of itself, and at.regular intervals resuming them all into itself again, in a general conflagration, in which perish all the gods and the otherwise immortal souls of men.

III. The Supreme Reason, which loves, but hates not, rules all phenomena by regular laws, in an Order of Nature to which there are no exceptions, even the human will being only the result of the motives, and thus so ordered as to fulfill the divine decrees.

IV. The Divine Providence allots to every creature all that is needed to make it happy, if it chooses to submit; and what seems evil, though necessary, is destined ultimately to pass away.

V. Happiness depends simply on virtue, which consists in consecration to the interests of mankind, who together form one brotherhood or universal city, and such service of humanity is the fundamental principle of morality, in obeying which we follow Nature and worship God, Our Father.

In short, Stoicism was not so much a philosophy as a religion. Its most characteristic utterance is the Hymn of Cleanthes, which has been given literally on page 63, but which is here repeated in a less prosaic form:

THE HYMN OF CLEANTHES.

FREELY TRANSLATED.

O Jove, of all the gods most high,
By many names men deify
Thy power supreme! All things obey
Thy laws; all nature 'feels thy sway.
We mortals should thy glory own,
For we're thy children; we alone,
Of living creatures, speech enjoy,
Thy reason's image: I'll employ
That speech in thine unceasing praise.
The universe thy will obeys,
And follows gladly thy command;
Resistless lightnings arm thy hand;
O'er all thou reignest in the might
Of reason's all-pervading light;
And naught is done without thy will
In heaven, earth, sea, except the ill

Which fools commit. But thou giv'st form
To what was formless; dost transform
Disorder into order; vile
Things turnest thou to precious; while
In harmony thy promptings draw
All on in one eternal law,
From which the wicked flee away,
But cannot thus impair its sway.
Ill-fated souls, their good in vain
They long for, who the sight disdain,
Or hearing, of thy laws, which give
To the obedient power to live
In happiness. But still astray
They go, each following his own way:
Some aiming after honors vain,
Some striving boundless wealth to gain,
Some seeking pleasure—all attain
A fate unlike the ends they strain
To reach. O Jove! who aye dost give
All good things, who in clouds dost live
And over lightnings rule, we crave
That man thou wouldst from folly save;
Oh, free his soul from error's night!
Oh, teach him how to gain the light
In which o'er nature thou hold'st sway,
That, being honored, we may pay
Thee honor in return; and tell
The grandeur of thy law, as well
Becomes us; gods nor men can raise
Themselves so high as when they praise.

And now I venture to subjoin, in illustration, not only of what Stoicism has been, but of what it may yet be, the following lines:

DAWN.

O thou who, out of darkness, mak'st thy throne,
I could not worship thee if thou wert known:
Then wert thou too like me, but now I see
Immeasurably thou transcendest me.
No human passion or caprice is seen
In thee. Thou art majestic and serene!
The chaos into Cosmos thou hast brought,
Raised worm to man, and instinct into thought:
From thee our thoughts, our wills, our feelings came,
Thou deathless heat, as we the flick'ring flame!
All beings urgest thou toward higher life,
As man thou'st raised from ignorance, lust, and strife,
To wisdom, order, purity, and love;
So still thou biddest us aspire above
This present to a future, grand and bright.
It dawns on me! Thanks, Power Unknown, there's light
Enough for me to toil to clear the way
In which some future man shall welcome day!

AUTHORITIES.

ANTONINUS. *The Thoughts of the Emperor Marcus Aurelius Antoninus.* Translated by George Long. London: Bell & Daldy. 1869. 1 vol., 8vo. (See, also, Fronto, Marc-Aurèle, and Theophrastus.)

ANTONINOS, MARKOS. *Ton eis Heauton Biblia.* A. Koraes (Coray). En Parisiois: Barrois. 1816. 1 vol., 8vo.

ARATUS. *Opera.* Recognovit Bekkerus. Berolini: Typis Reimeri. 1828. 1 vol., 8vo.

ARNOLD, MATTHEW. *Dramatic and Lyric Poems.* London: Macmillan & Co. 1869. 1 vol., 8vo.

BELIN DE BALLU. *Histoire Critique de l'Eloquence chez les Grecs.* Paris: A. Belin. 1813. 2 vols., 8vo.

CAPITOLINUS. *Scriptores Historiæ Romanæ Latini.* Edente Haurisio. Heidelbergæ: Hæner. 1743-48. 3 vols., folio.

CESAROTTI. *Opere, Corso di Letteratura Greca.* Firenze: Molini, Londi, e Comp. 1805. 3 vols., 8vo.

CHAMPIGNY. *Les Antonins.* Paris: Ambrose Bray. 1863. 3 vols, 18mo.

CICERO, M. T. *De Officiis.* Rec. Zumptius. Brunsvigæ. 1838. 1 vol., 8vo.

CICERO, M. T. *Opera.* Ex rec. Orellii. Turici (Zurich): Orellii. 1833–61. 8 vols., 8vo.

CLARKE, JAMES FREEMAN. *Ten Great Religions.* Boston: J. R. Osgood & Co. 1871. 1 vol., 8vo.

CLEANTHES. *Carmina, Fragmenta Philosophorum Græcorum.* Græce et Latini. Paris: Didot. 1860. 1 vol., 8vo. (See, also, Grant.)

COBBE, FRANCES POWER. *Essay on Intuitive Morals.* Boston: Crosby, Nichols & Co. 1859. 1 vol., 8vo.

DENIS. *Histoire des Théories et des Idées Morales dans l'Antiquité.* Paris: A. Durand. 1856. 2 vols., 8vo.

DIOGENES LAERTIUS. *Lives and Opinions of Eminent Philosophers.* Translated by C. D. Yonge. London: Henry G. Bohn. 1853. 1 vol., 8vo.

DION CASSIUS. *Historiæ Romanæ.* Rec. Reimarus. Hamburgi: Heroldi. 1750–52. 2 vols., folio.

DION CHRYSOSTOM. *Select Essays.* Translated by Gilbert Wakefield. London: R. Phillips. 1800. 1 vol., 8vo. (See, also, Jahn.)

DION CHRYSOSTOMUS. *Orationes.* Rec. Dindorfius. Lipsiae: Teubneri. 1857. 2 vols., 8vo.

DRUMANN. *Geschichte Roms nach Geschlechtern.* Königsberg: Bornträger. 1834–44. 6 vols., 8vo.

DRYDEN. *Miscellaneous Works.* [Translation from Persius.] London: Tonson. 1760. 4 vols., 8vo.

EPICTETUS. *Discourses, with the Enchiridion and Fragments.* Translated by George Long. London: George Bell & Sons. 1877. 1 vol., 8vo.

EPICTETUS. *Works.* A translation by Thomas Wentworth Higginson. Boston : Little, Brown & Co. 1866. 1 vol., 8vo.

EPIKTET. *Handbüchlein der Stoischen Moral.* Uebersetzt und erklärt von Carl Conz. Stuttgardt : Krais & Hoffmann. 1864. 1 vol., 8vo. (See, also, Theophrastus.)

FARRAR, Rev. F. W. *Seekers After God.* London : Macmillan & Co. 1868. 1 vol., 8vo.

FRANCKE, HEINRICH. *Zur Geschichte Trajan's.* Leipzig. 1840. 1 vol., 8vo.

FRONTO et MARCUS AURELIUS, Imperator. *Epistulæ.* Rec. Naber. Lipsiae : Teubnen. 1867. 1 vol., 8vo.

GRANT, Sir A. *Oxford Essays for 1858; Ancient Stoics* (with a translation of the Hymn of Cleanthes). London : J. W. Parker & Son. 1 vol.

HERODIAN : *His History.* Interpreted out of the Greek original by J. Maxwell. London : Hugh Perry. 1629. 1 vol., 4to.

JAHN, OTTO. *Aus der Alterthumswissenschaft* (for the translation from Dion Chrysostom). Bonn : Adolph Marcus. 1868. 1 vol., 8vo.

JULIAN. *Works.* Translated by John Duncombe. London : Codell. 1798. 2 vols., 8vo.

LACTANTIUS, F. *Opera.* Edidit Fritzsche. Lipsiæ : Tauchnitz. 1842. 1 vol., 8vo.

LECKY, W. E. H. *History of European Morals.* New York : D. Appleton & Co. 1869. 2 vols., 8vo.

LUCAN. *Pharsalia.* Translated into English verse by N. Rowe. London : Jacob Tonson. 1718. 1 vol., folio.

· LUCANUS. *Pharsalia.* Parisiis : Didot. An. Reipubl. III. 1795. 1 vol., folio.

MARC-AURELE. *Pensées.* Traduction d' Alexis Pierron. Deuxième edition. Paris : Charpentier. 1867. 1 vol., 12mo.

MARC-AURELE. *Pensées.* Traduction Nouvelle par J. Barthélemy-St. Hilaire. Paris : Germer-Baillière. 1876. 1 vol.

MARTHA, CHARLES. *Les Moralistes sur l'Empire Romain.* Paris : Hachette. 1872. 1 vol., 8vo.

MAURICE, F. D. *Moral and Metaphysical Philosophy.* London : Griffin & Co. 1850. 2 vols., 8vo.

MERIVALE, CHARLES. *History of the Romans Under the Empire.* New York : D. Appleton & Co. 1863-65. 7 vols.

MILL, JOHN STUART. *The Positive Philosophy of Auguste Comte.* Boston : William V. Spencer. 1867. 1 vol., 8vo.

MILL, JOHN STUART. *On Liberty.* New York : Henry Holt & Co. 1874. 1 vol., 8vo.

MILMAN, Rev. W. H. *History of Christianity.* London : John Murray. 1840. 3 vols., 8vo.

NIEBUHR, B. G. *Vorträge über Römische Geschichte.* Berlin : Reimer. 1846. 3 vols., 8vo.

PERSIUS, A. F. *Satiraræ.* Ex rec. Hermanni. Lipsiæ : Teubneri. 1859. 1 vol., 8vo.

PHILOSTRATUS *quæ Supersunt Omnia.* Rec. Olearius. Lipsiæ : Fritsch. 1709. 1 vol., folio.

PLATO. *The Dialogues.* Translated by B. Jowett. New York : Scribner, Armstrong & Co. 1873. 4 vols., 8vo.

PLINIUS, C. C. SECUNDUS. *Epistulæ.* Rec. Keil. Lipsiæ : Teubneri. 1865. 1 vol., 8vo.

PLUTARCH. *Lives.* Translation. Revised by A. H. Clough. Boston : Little, Brown & Co. 1859. 5 vols., 4to.

PLUTARCH. *Morals.* Translation. Revised by W. W. Goodwin. Boston : Little, Brown & Co. 1870. 5 vols., 8vo.

RITTER, Dr. A. H. *Geschichte der Philosophie.* Hamburg: Friedrich Perthes. 1829-53. 12 vols., 8vo.

SCHOELL, M. *Histoire de la Littérature Grecque Profane.* Paris: Gide Fils. 1824. 8 vols., 8vo.

SENECA. *Epistles.* Translated by Thomas Morell, LL.D. London: Woodfall. 1786. 2 vols., 4to.

SENECA, L. A. *Opera.* Rec. Haase. Lipsiæ: Teubneri. 1871. 3 vols., 8vo.

SENECA, L. A. *Tragœdiæ.* Rec. Schröderus. Delphis (Delft): Beman. 1728. 1 vol., 4to.

SENEQUE. *Œuvres, avec la traduction française de la collection Panckoucke.* Revue par M. Charpentier et M. Felix Lemaistre. Paris: Garnier Frères. 4 vols., 18mo.

STOBÆUS, J. *Florilegium.* Rec. Meinecke. Lipsiæ: Teubneri. 1855. 4 vols., 8vo.

STORY, W. W. *Castle St. Angelo and the Evil Eye.* London: Chapman & Hall; Philadelphia, J. B. Lippincott & Co. 1877. 1 vol., 8vo.

STORY, W. W. *A Conversation with Marcus Aurelius. Fortnightly Review* for February, 1873. New York: Holt & Williams. 1873.

TACITUS, C. C. *Works.* By Arthur Murphy. London: John Stockdale. 1807. 8 vols., 8vo.

TACITUS, C. C. *Scriptores Historiæ Romanæ Latini.* Edente Haurisio. Heidelbergæ: Hæner. 1743-48. 3 vols., folio. (Also, Vulcatius Gallicanus.)

TAINE, H. *Nouveaux Essais.* Marc-Aurèle. Paris: Hachette. 1866. 1 vol., 12mo.

TERENTIUS AFER, P. *Publ. Comœdiæ.* Parisiis: Typographia Regia. 1642. 1 vol., folio.

TERTULLIANUS, Q. S. F. *Writings.* Translated by Peter Holmes. Edinburgh : Clark. 1870. 3 vols., 8vo.

THEOPHRASTUS. *Characteres ; Marci Antonini Comment-arii ; Epicteti Dissertationes ab Arriano Literis Mandatæ, Fragmenta et Enchiridion.* Græce et Latine. Editore Didot. Parisiis : Didot. 1842. 1 vol., 8vo.

TRENCH, Archbishop. *Plutarch · His Life, His Lives, and His Morals ; Four Lectures.* London : Macmillan & Co. 1873. 1 vol., 8vo. (See, also, Julian, Fronto, Herodian.)

WEISS, JOHN. *Life and Correspondence of Theodore Parker.* New York : D. Appleton & Co. 1864. 2 vols., 8vo.

ZELLER, E. *The Stoics, Epicureans, and Sceptics.* Translated by O. J. Reichel. London : Longmans, Green & Co. 1870. 1 vol., 8vo.

INDEX.

P.

Lightning Source UK Ltd.
Milton Keynes UK
UKHW022214011020
370885UK00012B/333